Ajit Panicker is a firm believer in the boundless opportunities life offers to discover our true selves. Proudly identifying as a generalist rather than a super-specialist, he contends that super specialization is for unicellular organisms, not for evolved beings like humans.

As a distinguished author, Ajit has penned eleven books, with two becoming best-sellers. His latest work, "**Bossology: How to Manage Your Boss**," is a notable addition to the self-help genre.

Beyond his writing, Ajit is an **International Master Trainer & Facilitator specializing in Life Skills, a Motivational Speaker, and a Transformation Coach**. He is also the **founder of The SkillKrafter Academy**, a company dedicated to professional training and coaching services.

Ajit resides in Delhi with his supportive wife, Ratika, and their two children, Paarth and Aarika.

# THE FAILURE CODE

Ajit Panicker

ARPA PUBLICATIONS

ARPA Publications
Noida, Uttar Pardesh

First published by ARPA Publication in 2025



ISBN: 978-93-341-4932-6

1 0 9 8 7 6 5 4 3 2 1

# DEDICATION

This book is dedicated to all the resilient people around the world who never gave up. It is also dedicated to all who want to see themselves in the league of the above people - **The Resilient Superheroes.**

# EPIGRAPH

"I have not failed. I've just found 10,000 ways that won't work."

**— Thomas Edison**

# PREFACE

In the silent hours of the night, when doubts loom large and the weight of unmet dreams becomes unbearable, it's easy to see failure as a relentless enemy. We've all felt it—the bite of rejection, the pain of missed opportunities, and the haunting echo of "what ifs." This book, "**The Failure Code: A Success Formula That Never Fails**," emerged from those very shadows, born out of countless nights spent grappling with the fear of not being enough.

Imagine standing on the cliff of your aspirations, only to watch them crumble beneath your feet. It's a heart-wrenching experience, one that can leave you questioning your worth, your abilities, and your path. But what if I told you that within every failure lies a hidden blueprint for success? What if the very moments that brought you to your knees were the keys to unlocking a future more brilliant than you ever dared to dream?

"**The Failure Code**" is not just a book; it's a lifeline. It's a transformative guide that redefines how we perceive and navigate failure. Through powerful stories, practical strategies, and profound insights, this book invites you to embrace failure as an essential part of your journey. It shows you how to decode the messages hidden in your setbacks and turn them into stepping stones toward your ultimate success.

This book will change the way you look at failures in your life. It will teach you to see them not as endpoints but as pivotal moments of growth and learning. By delving into "**The Failure Code**," you'll discover the resilience within you, the strength to rise again, and the unwavering belief that success is not the absence of failure but the mastery of it.

Let "**The Failure Code**" be your guide to a life where failures are not feared but embraced, where every setback propels you forward, and where the formula for success is found in the heart of every fall. Embrace the code, unlock your potential, and discover a success formula that truly never fails.

■■■

# ACKNOWLEDGEMENT

Writing **"The Failure Code: A Success Formula That Never Fails"** has been a profound journey of reflection, growth, and resilience. This book is not merely a collection of thoughts but a testament to the power of perseverance and the lessons learned through the crucible of failure. It is with heartfelt gratitude that I acknowledge the incredible individuals and experiences that have made this book possible.

First and foremost, I extend my deepest appreciation to my family. Your unwavering support, encouragement, and love have been my foundation. To my parents, for instilling in me the values of hard work and determination; to my wife, Ratika for being my rock solid support and my source of inspiration; and to my children, Paarth and Aarika for reminding me of the boundless possibilities that lie ahead.

I am immensely grateful to my mentors and teachers, who have guided me with wisdom and insight. Your belief in my potential and your invaluable advice have been instrumental in shaping my journey. Thank you for pushing me to strive for excellence and for teaching me that failure is not an end but a beginning.

To my friends and colleagues, who have stood by me through thick and thin, thank you for your constant encouragement and for sharing in my dreams. Your faith in my vision and your honest feedback have been crucial in the development of this book.

I am profoundly thankful to the individuals whose stories and experiences have enriched these pages. Your courage to share your struggles and triumphs has been a source of inspiration and a reminder that we are all connected by the thread of human resilience.

A special thank you to my editor and the entire publishing team. Your expertise, dedication, and meticulous attention to detail have brought this book to life. Your partnership has been invaluable, and I am grateful for your unwavering commitment to excellence.

Finally, to my readers, thank you for embarking on this journey with me. It is my hope that **"The Failure Code"** will inspire you to view failures through a new lens and to embrace them as stepping stones to your greatest successes. Your willingness to explore and grow is the true heart of this book.

With deep gratitude,
**__Ajit Panicker**

■■■

# TABLE OF CONTENTS

# CHAPTER 1

## UNDERSTANDING THE FAILURE CODE

# THE MYTH OF FAILURE

In the world of success and personal development, there is a pervasive myth that failure is something to be feared and avoided at all costs. From a young age, we are conditioned to view failure as a sign of weakness or incompetence, and we are encouraged to do everything in our power to prevent it from happening.

But what if I told you that failure is not only inevitable but also necessary for growth and success? What if I told you that failure is actually a key ingredient in the recipe for achieving your goals and living your best life?

The truth is, failure is not the end of the road—it is simply a detour on the path to success.

> *In my years of working in corporate environments with professionals, I have repeatedly seen how those who embrace failure as a learning opportunity are the ones who go on to achieve great things. They understand that failure is not a reflection of their worth or abilities but simply a stepping stone on the journey to greatness.*

Consider the world of business. **Steve Jobs, co-founder of Apple**, faced a highly publicized failure when he was ousted from his own company in 1985. Instead of giving up, he founded NeXT and acquired Pixar, which led to revolutionary successes. His return to Apple marked a period of unprecedented innovation and success for the company. In India, **Dhirubhai Ambani, the founder of Reliance Industries**, faced numerous setbacks and failures in his journey from a petrol station attendant to a business tycoon. His ability to learn from failures and persevere led to the creation of one of India's largest conglomerates.

In politics, **Abraham Lincoln** is a quintessential example. Before becoming the 16th President of the United States, he faced multiple electoral defeats and personal failures. His resilience and determination through these failures ultimately led him to lead the nation through its Civil War and abolish slavery. In India, **Prime Minister Narendra Modi** faced several criticisms, allegations and political obstacles before rising to national prominence, showcasing how persistence in the face of failure can lead to significant political success.

In sports, **Michael Jordan**, widely regarded as one of the greatest basketball players of all time, was cut from his high school basketball team. He has famously said, "I've missed more than 9,000 shots in my career. I've lost almost 300 games. Twenty-six times, I've been trusted to take the game-winning shot and missed. I've failed over and over and over again in my life. And that is why I succeed." In cricket, **Sachin Tendulkar**, despite numerous setbacks and failures, became one of the greatest batsmen in history, breaking multiple records and inspiring millions.

The key to overcoming obstacles and achieving success lies in shifting your mindset from one of fear and avoidance to one of resilience and growth. Instead of seeing failure as a roadblock, see it as a sign that you are pushing yourself outside of your comfort zone and challenging yourself to reach new heights. Embrace failure as a teacher, not a punishment, and use it as an opportunity to learn, grow, and improve.

So the next time you encounter a setback or stumble on your path to success, remember that failure is not a mark of shame but a badge of honour. It means you are daring greatly, taking risks, and refusing to settle for mediocrity. Trust in **The Failure Code: a success formula that never fails.** With the right mindset and motivation, you can overcome any obstacle that stands in your way.

Let go of the myth of failure and embrace the power of resilience, determination, and growth. You are capable of achieving greatness—all you have to do is believe in yourself and keep pushing forward.

■■

# THE IMPORTANCE OF FAILURE IN SUCCESS

Failure is often seen as a negative outcome, something to be avoided at all costs. However, in reality, failure is a crucial stepping stone on the path to success. In my book, "**The Failure Code: A Success Formula That Never Fails**," I highlight the importance of failure in achieving your goals and reaching your full potential. It is through failure that you learn valuable lessons, build resilience, and ultimately grow stronger.

In the world of **The Failure Code**, failure is not something to be feared, but rather embraced as a necessary part of the journey towards success. It is through our failures that we gain valuable insight into what works and what doesn't, allowing us to make necessary adjustments and improvements. By viewing failure as a learning opportunity rather than a setback, you can turn your mistakes into stepping stones toward your goal.

Personal development is all about pushing ourselves out of our comfort zones and challenging ourselves to grow. Failure is an essential part of this process, as it forces us to confront our limitations and push past them. By embracing failure and using it as a tool for personal growth, you can unlock your full potential and achieve greater success in both your personal and professional lives.

Overcoming obstacles is a key component of success, and failure is often the biggest obstacle we face. By learning to navigate through failure and bounce back stronger, you can overcome any challenge that comes your way. With the right mindset and motivation, you can turn your failures into fuel for success, propelling you towards your goals with renewed determination and resilience.

*My own journey is a testament to the power of embracing failure. I once aspired to become a Naval Fighter Pilot, but my dreams took a different turn. After transitioning to the corporate world, I started as a Sales Officer selling cars. I faced numerous setbacks, but each failure taught me valuable lessons. Eventually, I moved into consultative selling as a Banker and Certified Financial Planner. To do something greater than what I was doing, I took risk and ventured on my entrepreneurial journey. However, my entrepreneurial venture, CELEB FINANCIAL PLANNERS PVT LTD, shut down in just 2.5 years. This failure was a significant blow, but it became the foundation for my future success.*

Instead of letting this setback define me, I used it as a learning experience. I rebuilt my career, becoming a Sales Trainer, Life Skills Trainer, Team Building Trainer, Leadership Trainer, and Author of 11 books. Each failure along the way equipped me with the resilience and insights needed to succeed in these roles.

So, failure is not something to be feared or avoided but rather embraced as a necessary part of the journey towards success. By viewing failure as a learning opportunity, you can turn your mistakes into valuable lessons that propel you toward your goals. With the right mindset and motivation, you can overcome any obstacle that comes your way and achieve greater success than you ever thought possible. Embrace failure, learn from it, and watch as it becomes the key to unlocking your full potential.

■■

# UNPACKING THE FAILURE CODE

In this chapter, we will delve into the concepts of **The Failure Code** and explore how it can be unpacked and understood to pave the way for your success in life, both at personal and professional levels. **The Failure Code** is not just a set of rules or guidelines, but rather a powerful formula that has the potential to transform failure into success. By understanding and applying this code, you can overcome obstacles and achieve your goals with ease.

One of the biggest obstacles that working professionals face is the fear of failure. However, by unpacking **The Failure Code**, you can learn to embrace failure as a stepping stone toward success. Failure is not the end, but rather an opportunity for growth and learning. By changing your mindset and viewing failure as a valuable experience, you can overcome your fears and achieve your goals with confidence and determination.

**The Failure Code** can serve as a roadmap for personal development, guiding professionals toward success in their careers and personal lives. Personal development is the key to cracking **The Failure Code**. It is important for us to constantly strive for self-improvement and growth in order to reach our full potential. By adopting a growth mindset and focusing on continuous learning and development, we can unlock our true talents and capabilities.

Mindset and motivation play a crucial role in cracking **The Failure Code**. It is important for working professionals to cultivate a positive and resilient mindset that can withstand challenges and setbacks. By staying motivated and focusing on your goals, you can overcome any obstacle that comes your way. **The Failure Code** provides the tools and strategies needed to maintain a strong mindset and stay motivated in the face of adversity.

Real people who have successfully unpacked **The Failure Code** and implemented the have transformed their lives completely. Let's look at a few examples who could unpack this potent code:

## Steve Jobs' Comeback

Steve Jobs, the co-founder of Apple, faced a highly publicized failure when he was ousted from his own company in 1985. Instead of giving up, he founded NeXT and acquired Pixar, which led to revolutionary successes. His return to Apple marked a period of unprecedented innovation and success for the company. Jobs embraced failure as a learning experience, which allowed him to make necessary adjustments and achieve greater success.

## J.K. Rowling's Transformation

Before J.K. Rowling became one of the world's most famous authors, she faced numerous rejections and personal hardships. Her manuscript for "Harry Potter and the Philosopher's Stone" was rejected by multiple publishers before being accepted. Rowling's ability to view these rejections as opportunities for growth and refinement allowed her to create a beloved book series that has inspired millions.

## Thomas Edison's Persistence

Thomas Edison, one of the greatest inventors in history, failed thousands of times before successfully inventing the electric light bulb. Edison's perspective on failure was that each unsuccessful attempt was a step closer to finding a solution. His resilience and determination exemplify the power of embracing failure as part of the journey to success.

## MS Dhoni's Cricket Career

MS Dhoni, one of India's most successful cricket captains, faced numerous setbacks in his early career. From being an Indian Railways Ticket Examiner to the Legend in Leadership in the world of sports, he has a come a long way. Despite these early failures, Dhoni's resilience and calm under pressure led India to win the T20 World Cup in 2007, the ICC Cricket World Cup in 2011, and the Champions Trophy in 2013. Dhoni's ability to learn from his failures and lead by example turned him into a legendary figure in cricket.

## Rohit Sharma's Rise

Rohit Sharma, now one of the most prolific batsmen in cricket, had a rocky start to his international career. Inconsistent performances led to him being dropped from the team multiple times. However, Sharma's determination to improve and his willingness to learn from his failures saw him evolve into a reliable opener, setting records and leading the Indian cricket team to numerous victories. Finally, being able to win a T-20 World Cup for India in 2024.

## Sunil Chhetri's Football Journey

Sunil Chhetri, India's football captain and one of the highest goal-scorers in international football, faced significant challenges early in his career, including limited opportunities and initial failures at international clubs. Chhetri's perseverance and constant effort to improve his game have made him an inspiration for aspiring footballers, proving that failures can be stepping stones to achieving greatness.

## Satya Nadella's Leadership at Microsoft

Satya Nadella, the CEO of Microsoft, encountered numerous challenges and setbacks throughout his career. Under his leadership, Microsoft underwent a significant transformation, shifting focus to cloud computing and AI, which revitalized the company's fortunes. Nadella's ability to embrace failure, learn from it, and innovate has made him a renowned leader in the tech industry.

Unpacking **The Failure Code** is essential for working professionals who are seeking success in their careers and personal lives. By understanding and applying this powerful formula, you can overcome obstacles, develop a growth mindset, and stay motivated in the face of failure. **The Failure Code** is a success formula that never fails, and by embracing it, you can unlock your full potential and achieve your goals with confidence and determination.

■■■

# CHAPTER 2

# PERSONAL DEVELOPMENT FOR SUCCESS

# SETTING CLEAR GOALS

Setting clear goals is an essential step in achieving success in both your personal and professional life. Without clear goals, it can be easy to lose focus and become overwhelmed by the obstacles that come your way. In order to truly crack **The Failure Code**, you must first define what success looks like for you and set specific, measurable goals to help you get there.

## The Importance of Setting Clear Goals

One of the key components of **The Failure Code** is having a clear vision of what you want to achieve. By setting specific goals, you are able to create a roadmap for success and stay motivated even when faced with challenges. Without clear goals, it can be easy to lose sight of your ultimate objective and become discouraged when things don't go as planned.

Setting clear goals helps you in multiple ways:

- **Focus:** It allows you to concentrate your efforts on what truly matters, avoiding distractions.
- **Motivation:** Clear goals provide a sense of direction and purpose, keeping you motivated.
- **Measurement:** Goals give you benchmarks to measure your progress, helping you stay on track.
- **Resilience:** By having clear goals, you can better navigate setbacks and failures, using them as learning opportunities rather than roadblocks.

## The GOALS Model

To effectively set clear goals, you can use the GOALS model as a guide. This model will help you ensure that your goals are well-defined and actionable. GOALS stands for:

1. **G**oal: Define your objective clearly.
2. **O**bservable: Ensure your goal is measurable.
3. **A**chievable: Set realistic and attainable goals.
4. **L**inear: Break down your goal into manageable steps.
5. **S**ustainable: Make sure your goal is sustainable over time.

## Using the GOALS Model

### 1. Goal: Define Your Objective Clearly

The first step is to clearly define what you want to achieve. Be specific about your objective. For example, instead of saying "I want to be successful," define what success means to you. It could be "I want to become a team leader in my department within the next year."

### 2. Observable: Ensure Your Goal is Measurable

Make sure your goal is measurable so you can track your progress. Use quantifiable metrics. For instance, if your goal is to improve your sales performance, specify how much you want to increase your sales by, such as "I want to increase my sales by 20% in the next six months."

### 3. Achievable: Set Realistic and Attainable Goals

Your goals should be challenging yet realistic. Setting unattainable goals can lead to frustration and discouragement. Evaluate your current situation and resources to ensure your goals are achievable. For example, if you aim to learn a new skill, set a goal that considers your current knowledge and available time.

### 4. Linear: Break Down Your Goal into Manageable Steps

Break down your goal into smaller, manageable tasks. This makes it less overwhelming and allows you to make steady progress. For instance, if your goal is to write a book, break it down into steps like outlining the chapters, writing a certain number of pages per day, and revising each chapter.

**5. Sustainable: Make Sure Your Goal is Sustainable Over Time**

Ensure that your goal is sustainable and can be maintained over time. Consider the long-term implications and how you can continue to achieve and maintain your goal. For example, if your goal is to adopt a healthier lifestyle, create a plan that incorporates balanced nutrition and regular exercise that you can sustain in the long run.

## Implementing the GOALS Model

By following the **GOALS model**, you can set clear, actionable goals that will guide you towards success. Here's an example of how you might apply this model:

- **G:** I want to become a project manager in my company.
- **O:** I will complete a project management certification and lead at least one project within the next year.
- **A:** I will dedicate 10 hours per week to studying and apply for project management roles within my company.
- **L:** I will break down my study plan into weekly topics and set milestones for applying to roles.
- **S:** I will maintain a balanced workload to ensure I can keep up with my certification and job responsibilities.

Setting clear goals is a crucial step in cracking **The Failure Code** and achieving success. By defining what success looks like for you, breaking down your goals into smaller tasks, and maintaining a positive mindset, you are able to overcome obstacles and reach your full potential.

Remember, success is within reach for all working professionals who are willing to put in the effort and stay focused on their goals.

Embrace the **GOALS model**, and watch as it transforms your approach to personal and professional development.

# DEVELOPING A GROWTH MINDSET

In order to achieve success in both your personal and professional life, it is essential to develop a growth mindset. A growth mindset is the belief that your abilities and intelligence can be developed through hard work, perseverance, and dedication. This mindset is crucial for overcoming obstacles and achieving your goals, no matter how big or small they may be.

## Understanding the Growth Mindset

The concept of the growth mindset was popularized by psychologist Carol Dweck. **According to Dweck, individuals with a growth mindset believe that their talents and abilities can be developed through effort, good strategies, and input from others. In contrast, those with a fixed mindset believe that their talents and abilities are static and unchangeable.**

One of the key components of developing a growth mindset is embracing failure as a learning opportunity. This is at the heart of **The Failure Code**. Instead of viewing setbacks as permanent roadblocks, see them as stepping stones on the path to success. By learning from your failures and using them to grow and improve, you will be better equipped to overcome future challenges and reach your full potential.

## The Role of Failure in a Growth Mindset

In her research, Dweck found that people with a growth mindset are more likely to view failures as opportunities to learn and grow. They understand that failure is not a reflection of their worth or capabilities but rather a natural part of the learning process. This perspective, which is integral to **The Failure Code**, allows them to persist in the face of adversity and continue striving towards their goals.

For example, consider the story of Thomas Edison, who famously said, "I have not failed. I've just found 10,000 ways that won't work." Edison's resilience and willingness to learn from his failures ultimately led to the invention of the light bulb. By adopting a similar attitude, you can transform your setbacks into valuable experiences that contribute to your growth and development, aligning perfectly with the principles of **The Failure Code**.

## Embracing a Growth Mindset

To develop a growth mindset, it is important to cultivate a positive attitude and believe in your own abilities. By fostering a sense of self-belief and confidence, you will be more likely to take risks, push yourself out of your comfort zone, and pursue your goals with determination and perseverance.

Here are some strategies to help you embrace a growth mindset, all of which are part of **The Failure Code**:

1. **View Challenges as Opportunities:** Instead of avoiding difficult tasks, see them as chances to learn and grow. Embrace the challenge and give it your best effort.
2. **Learn from Criticism:** Constructive feedback is invaluable for growth. Rather than taking criticism personally, use it as a tool for improvement.
3. **Celebrate Effort, Not Just Success:** Recognize and celebrate the hard work and effort you put into achieving your goals, regardless of the outcome. This reinforces the importance of persistence and dedication.
4. **Be Persistent:** Understand that success often requires time and sustained effort. Stay committed to your goals, even when progress seems slow.
5. **Cultivate Resilience:** Develop the ability to bounce back from setbacks. Use failures as opportunities to learn and adapt your strategies.

## The Importance of Support Systems

In order to truly develop a growth mindset, it is essential to surround yourself with positive influences and support systems. Seek out mentors, coaches, and like-minded individuals who can provide guidance, encouragement, and motivation as you work towards your goals. By surrounding yourself with people who believe in you and your potential, you will be better equipped to overcome obstacles, stay motivated, and continue on your path to success.

For instance, think about the support networks that athletes often rely on. A professional tennis player, for example, might have a coach, a fitness trainer, a nutritionist, and a sports psychologist. Each member of the team plays a crucial role in helping the athlete improve and stay focused on their goals. Similarly, building a supportive network in your personal and professional life can significantly enhance your growth mindset and help you implement **The Failure Code**.

## Examples of Growth Mindset in Popular Personalities

Many well-known personalities from India and around the world exemplify the growth mindset. For instance:

- **MS Dhoni (India, Cricket):** Known for his calm demeanour and resilience, Dhoni has led his team to numerous victories by learning from defeats and continuously improving.
- **Rohit Sharma (India, Cricket):** His journey from being an inconsistent player to one of the best batsmen in the world is a testament to his growth mindset.
- **Sunil Chhetri (India, Football):** As one of the most successful Indian footballers, Chhetri's perseverance and continuous self-improvement have set him apart.

- **Satya Nadella (India, Microsoft CEO):** Nadella's leadership at Microsoft is marked by a culture of learning and growth, driving the company to new heights.
- **Oprah Winfrey (USA, Media Mogul):** Overcoming numerous personal and professional setbacks, Winfrey's growth mindset has made her one of the most influential women in the world.
- **Elon Musk (USA, Entrepreneur):** Musk's ventures, from SpaceX to Tesla, have faced significant failures, but his resilience and continuous learning have led to ground breaking successes.

Developing a growth mindset is essential for achieving success in both your personal and professional life. By embracing failure as a learning opportunity, believing in your own abilities, maintaining a positive attitude, and surrounding yourself with positive influences, you will be better equipped to overcome obstacles, achieve your goals, and reach your full potential.

Remember, success is not about avoiding failure but about learning from it, growing from it, and using it to propel yourself towards greater heights.

Embrace the growth mindset, and watch as it transforms your approach to personal and professional development, all in alignment with **The Failure Code**.

■■

## CONTINUOUS LEARNING AND DEVELOPMENT

Continuous learning and improvement are essential components of success in both personal and professional life. As working professionals, we must constantly strive to expand our knowledge and skills to stay ahead in our careers. **The Failure Code** offers a success formula that never fails, and at the heart of this formula is the belief in the power of continuous learning and improvement.

Personal development is a lifelong journey that requires a commitment to growth and self-improvement. By continuously learning and seeking out new opportunities to expand our skills and knowledge, we can position ourselves for success in our careers. **The Failure Code** reminds us that obstacles are simply opportunities for growth. By embracing challenges and setbacks, we can become stronger and more resilient professionals.

## Real-Life Examples of Continuous Learning you will immediately relate to:

### Sachin Tendulkar

Sachin Tendulkar, one of the greatest cricketers of all time, exemplifies the principle of continuous learning and improvement. Despite his immense talent, Tendulkar never stopped honing his skills. After experiencing a slump in form, he would analyse his game, seek advice from coaches and peers, and make necessary adjustments. His commitment to learning and improvement kept him at the top of his game for over two decades.

### Virat Kohli

Virat Kohli, another cricket legend, transformed himself from a promising young player into one of the best batsmen in the world through relentless learning and improvement. Kohli faced a period when his fitness was becoming a reason for not being able to continue for long. That's when he learned to be at the top of the game, his fitness has to be at the top most level. He faced a lean period from 2019 until 2023 not being able to score hundreds and getting out soon. But he kept learning and kept improving by learning the mistakes he was making. He focused on his fitness, refined his technique, and sought mentorship, turning his failures into stepping stones for success.

### Rahul Dravid

Known as "The Wall" of Indian cricket, Rahul Dravid's career is a testament to the power of continuous improvement. Dravid faced criticism for his slow scoring rate early in his career. Instead of being discouraged, he worked on his weaknesses and adapted his game to different formats of cricket. His dedication to learning and improving made him one of the most dependable players in cricket history.

## Elon Musk

In the business world, Elon Musk is a prime example of how continuous learning and improvement can lead to extraordinary success. Musk faced numerous failures with SpaceX, including multiple rocket launch failures. However, he never let these setbacks deter him. Instead, he and his team analyzed each failure, learned from their mistakes, and made improvements. This relentless pursuit of knowledge and improvement led SpaceX to become a pioneer in space exploration.

**The Failure Code** emphasizes that continuous learning and improvement should be the next step after failures. This involves reflection and introspection to understand what went wrong and how to improve. By adopting this approach, failures can be transformed into valuable learning experiences that drive future success.

Our mindset and motivation play a crucial role in our ability to continuously learn and improve. By maintaining a positive attitude and staying motivated to reach our goals, we can overcome any obstacles that stand in our way. **The Failure Code** encourages us to stay focused on our personal development and to never stop striving for excellence in our careers.

Continuous learning and improvement are essential components of success for working professionals. By embracing **The Failure Code**'s success formula and committing to personal development, we can overcome obstacles, adopt a growth mindset, and stay motivated to achieve our goals.

Remember that success is not a destination, but a journey of continuous growth and improvement.

By learning from the experiences of personalities like Sachin Tendulkar, Virat Kohli, Rahul Dravid, and Elon Musk, we can see how embracing continuous learning and improvement can lead to remarkable success.

**The Failure Code** reminds us that with the right mindset, every failure is an opportunity for growth, and every challenge is a chance to improve.

■■■

# CHAPTER 3

## OVERCOMING OBSTACLES IN THE WORK PLACE

# IDENTIFYING COMMON WORKPLACE OBSTACLES

In the journey toward success, every working professional will inevitably encounter obstacles. Recognizing these challenges is crucial for overcoming them and achieving your goals. While some obstacles are more evident, others can be subtle but equally impactful. This chapter explores common workplace obstacles that does not let you succeed.

## Common Workplace Obstacles

1. **Lack of Motivation**: One of the most prevalent obstacles is a lack of motivation. It's easy to become disengaged or complacent amidst the routine of daily work. When motivation wanes, productivity and enthusiasm can suffer, leading to stagnation. Identifying this decline early and taking proactive steps to rekindle your passion can help you push past this barrier.
2. **Fear of Failure**: The fear of failure can paralyze individuals, preventing them from taking risks or stepping out of their comfort zones. This fear often stems from the worry of not meeting expectations or facing judgment. However, understanding that failure is not the end but a crucial learning opportunity can shift your perspective. Embracing this mindset allows you to tackle challenges head-on and grow from your experiences.
3. **External Challenges**: Difficult colleagues, toxic work environments, and organizational issues can also impede success. Navigating these external challenges requires tact and resilience. Whether it involves setting healthy boundaries, seeking support from mentors, or addressing workplace toxicity, identifying these issues and taking constructive actions is vital for maintaining a positive work

environment.

4. **Poor Communication**: Miscommunication or lack of communication can lead to misunderstandings, conflicts, and inefficiencies. Effective communication is essential for collaboration and productivity. Identifying communication gaps and working to improve clarity and understanding can help in mitigating this obstacle.
5. **Inadequate Resources**: Sometimes, the lack of necessary resources—whether it's time, budget, or tools—can hinder performance and progress. Recognizing these constraints and advocating for what you need can be crucial in overcoming this challenge.
6. **Resistance to Change**: In a dynamic work environment, resistance to change can be a significant obstacle. Adapting to new processes, technologies, or organizational shifts can be challenging. Understanding the benefits of change and being open to adaptation can help in navigating this hurdle.
7. **Work-Life Imbalance**: Balancing professional responsibilities with personal life is another common challenge. Overworking or neglecting personal time can lead to burnout and reduced effectiveness. Identifying and addressing work-life balance issues can help maintain overall well-being and productivity.

It is important for working professionals to identify these challenges and take proactive steps to address them. Whether it be setting boundaries with colleagues or seeking support from a mentor, there are always ways to overcome these external obstacles and create a more positive and productive work environment.

By identifying and overcoming these common workplace obstacles, professionals can unlock their full potential and achieve their goals.

The key is to have the right mindset and motivation to push past these challenges and never give up on the path to success.

Remember, with the right mindset and determination, there is no obstacle that cannot be overcome on the journey to achieving your dreams.

■■

# STRATEGIES FOR OVERCOMING WORKPLACE CHALLENGES

In the fast-paced world of the modern workplace, obstacles are inevitable. However, it is our response to these challenges that defines our success. Understanding and overcoming these common workplace obstacles can transform setbacks into opportunities for growth and achievement.

In this chapter, we will explore how to effectively address these challenges using the model **MOTIVATES** and how I have applied this approach to overcome obstacles in my career.

## MOTIVATES: Overcoming Workplace Obstacles

**Motivation Loss:** One of the most prevalent challenges professionals face is a loss of motivation. It's easy to become disengaged or complacent in the daily grind of work. To counteract this, regularly revisit your goals and achievements. Set short-term milestones to keep yourself energized and focused. For me, maintaining motivation required revisiting my career goals regularly and celebrating small victories, which kept me driven even during challenging times.

**O**bstructive Fear: Fear of failure can prevent us from taking necessary risks and stepping out of our comfort zones. Embrace failure as a learning opportunity rather than a roadblock. When I faced setbacks early in my career, I shifted my perspective to view them as valuable lessons, which empowered me to take calculated risks and innovate in my roles.

**T**oxic Environment: A negative work environment or difficult colleagues can hinder productivity and morale. Address these external challenges by setting clear boundaries and seeking support when needed. In my experience, navigating a toxic environment involved building strong, supportive relationships with positive colleagues and seeking mentorship to provide guidance and encouragement.

Ineffective Communication: Poor communication can lead to misunderstandings and inefficiencies. Strive for clear, open dialogue and ensure you're actively listening. Enhancing communication skills became crucial for me, as I took courses and worked with mentors to improve my ability to convey ideas effectively and build better team dynamics.

Vital Resources Shortage: Sometimes, a lack of essential resources—be it time, budget, or tools—can impede progress. Advocate for the resources you need and prioritize tasks effectively. I learned to manage resource constraints by prioritizing tasks and negotiating for necessary tools, which allowed me to maintain productivity and achieve project goals.

Adaptability Issues: Resistance to change can stall progress. Cultivate a flexible mindset and adapt to new processes or organizational shifts. Embracing change became a cornerstone of my career development. When faced with significant changes, I approached them with an open mind and actively sought ways to integrate new strategies into my work.

Time Management: Balancing professional responsibilities with personal life is crucial to avoid burnout. Develop effective time management strategies and set realistic goals. I found that organizing my schedule and setting clear priorities helped me manage my time better, leading to improved efficiency and work-life balance.

External Pressures: Market demands or organizational changes can create additional stress. Stay resilient and focus on your core objectives. During high-pressure periods, I maintained my focus on long-term goals and used stress-management techniques to stay calm and productive.

Stagnation: Periods of stagnation can lead to decreased motivation and Innovation. Inject new energy into your work by seeking fresh perspectives and setting new challenges. To overcome stagnation, I actively sought out new projects and roles that pushed me beyond my comfort zone, which rejuvenated my enthusiasm and drive.

■■

## APPLYING THE FAILURE CODE

By incorporating **The Failure Code**, you can view these obstacles as opportunities for growth. Embrace failure as a crucial part of your journey, continuously invest in personal development, and maintain a positive mindset. Surround yourself with supportive colleagues and mentors who can provide encouragement and guidance.

Throughout my career, applying the **MOTIVATES** framework has been instrumental in overcoming various obstacles. Each challenge I faced was an opportunity to apply new strategies, learn from experiences, and ultimately, achieve success.

Remember, overcoming workplace challenges requires a blend of mindset, development, and motivation. By embracing these principles, you can navigate even the most difficult obstacles with resilience and grace.

Embrace challenges as opportunities in disguise, learn from them, and watch as you soar to new heights of success in your career.

■■

## BUILDING RESILIENCE IN THE FACE OF ADVERSITY

In the fast-paced modern workplace, facing adversity is not just a possibility—it's a certainty. How we respond to these challenges often defines our success. Building resilience is crucial to navigate the ups and downs of our careers and personal lives, transforming setbacks into stepping stones for growth. This aligns seamlessly with **The Failure Code**, which emphasizes that failure is not the end but a critical component of the path to success.

**RESILIENCE** is not merely about enduring difficulties; it's about converting them into opportunities for advancement. To build resilience effectively and integrate it with **The Failure Code**, consider the framework **RESILIENCE** as a strategic guide:

**<u>REFLECT ON CHALLENGES</u>**: Recognize and analyze the adversity you face. Understanding the nature of these challenges allows you to address them more effectively. **The Failure Code** teaches us that reflecting on what went wrong helps us adapt and improve. I applied this principle by thoroughly evaluating project failures to identify weaknesses and implement corrective actions.

**<u>EMBRACE LEARNING</u>:** View each setback as a learning opportunity. **The Failure Code** highlights the importance of using failure as a learning tool rather than a defeat. Embracing this perspective helped me and many others to continuously refine our skills and strategies, transforming setbacks into valuable lessons.

**<u>STRENGTHEN EMOTIONAL INTELLIGENCE</u>**: Develop emotional intelligence to manage stress and enhance communication during tough times. This aligns with **The Failure Code**'s focus on personal development and growth. Improving emotional intelligence enabled me to handle stress better and communicate more effectively, crucial for overcoming workplace challenges.

**<u>INVEST IN PERSONAL GROWTH</u>**: Dedicate time to continuous personal and professional development. **The Failure Code** underscores that growth is a lifelong journey. Investing in learning new skills and seeking mentorship fortified my resilience and adaptability, essential for navigating career obstacles.

**<u>LEVERAGE SUPPORT SYSTEMS</u>**: Build and rely on a network of supportive colleagues, mentors, and friends. According to **The Failure Code**, having a support system is vital for overcoming challenges. My network provided invaluable perspectives and encouragement, which bolstered my resilience and motivation during tough times.

**<u>INITIATE PROBLEM-SOLVING</u>**: Engage actively in problem-solving when facing obstacles. **The Failure Code** encourages proactive approaches to overcoming challenges. Tackling problems head-on with creativity and a solution-oriented mindset helped me and my team navigate difficulties more effectively.

**<u>ESTABLISH CLEAR GOALS</u>**: Set specific, achievable goals to maintain focus and direction despite setbacks. **The Failure Code** emphasizes the importance of clear goals as a motivational tool. By defining and pursuing clear objectives, I maintained direction and motivation, even through challenging periods.

**NURTURE A POSITIVE MINDSET**: Cultivate optimism and resilience. **The Failure Code** advocates for a positive mindset to navigate obstacles. Maintaining a positive attitude allowed me to approach challenges with renewed energy and determination, reinforcing the idea that setbacks are opportunities for growth.

**CELEBRATE SMALL WINS**: Recognize and celebrate minor achievements along the way. **The Failure Code** highlights the importance of acknowledging progress to boost morale. Celebrating small victories helped keep the team motivated and focused on overcoming larger challenges.

**EXAMINE AND ADJUST**: Regularly review and adjust your strategies based on feedback and results. Flexibility is a key aspect of **The Failure Code**. By examining what works and adjusting strategies, I could continuously refine my approach, improving resilience in future challenges.

## Applying RESILIENCE Framework: The Failure Code

Building resilience is a vital component of **The Failure Code**, which encourages transforming failures into growth opportunities. By applying the **RESILIENCE** framework, you align with the core principles of **The Failure Code**: viewing failure as a learning tool, continuously improving, and maintaining a positive mindset.

Every setback is a chance to grow and develop further. Embracing challenges as opportunities to build resilience, while integrating **The Failure Code**'s principles, ensures that you turn obstacles into stepping stones toward success. With the right mindset and strategies, you can overcome any challenge and achieve success in your career and personal life.

■■■

# CHAPTER 4

# CULTIVATING A SUCCESS MINDSET

# THE POWER OF POSITIVE THINKING

In the fast-paced world of today's workplace, the power of positive thinking is not just a desirable trait but a crucial component of success. Embracing a positive mindset is integral to navigating the ups and downs of your career and personal life, and it is a core element of **The Failure Code**, a success formula that never fails. **The Failure Code** emphasizes that maintaining a positive outlook, even in the face of adversity, can transform setbacks into opportunities and drive long-term success.

**POSITIVE THINKING** is a strategic approach that aligns perfectly with the principles of **The Failure Code**. It helps you view challenges and setbacks as opportunities for growth rather than insurmountable obstacles. By adopting a positive mindset, you not only improve your resilience but also set yourself up for future success. Here's how the framework **POSITIVE** encapsulates the essence of positive thinking within **The Failure Code**:

**PERCEPTION SHIFT**: **The Failure Code** teaches us that altering our perception of challenges is crucial. Instead of seeing setbacks as failures, view them as valuable learning experiences. This shift helps you stay focused on your goals and turn obstacles into stepping stones.

**OPTIMISM**: Maintaining an optimistic outlook aligns with **The Failure Code**'s emphasis on positivity. Believing in positive outcomes keeps you motivated and enthusiastic, which is essential for persevering through difficulties and achieving success.

**SELF-BELIEF**: **The Failure Code** underscores the importance of self-belief. Confidence in your abilities fuels your determination and helps you overcome obstacles. Trusting in your potential allows you to push through challenges and stay on the path to success.

**INSPIRATION**: Drawing inspiration from both your achievements and those of others supports **The Failure Code**'s philosophy.

Inspiration provides the motivation needed to tackle new challenges and reinforces the idea that success is a continuous journey of growth.

**TENACITY**: Demonstrating tenacity is a fundamental aspect of **The Failure Code**. A positive mindset fosters persistence, enabling you to overcome obstacles and remain committed to your goals, even when faced with setbacks.

**INTEGRATION**: Integrating positive thinking into your daily routine aligns with **The Failure Code**'s principles of continuous improvement. Making positivity a habit enhances your ability to handle challenges and maintain focus on your objectives.

**VISION**: Keeping a clear vision of your goals is essential in **The Failure Code**. A positive mindset helps you stay focused on your long-term objectives, guiding you through obstacles and ensuring that you remain aligned with your ultimate aspirations.

**EMPOWERMENT**: Empowering yourself and those around you through positivity is a key element of **The Failure Code**. Building a supportive and encouraging environment strengthens collective resilience and drives success.

## Applying POSITIVE Thinking in The Failure Code

The power of positive thinking is a cornerstone of **The Failure Code**'s success formula. By embracing the **POSITIVE** approach, you align with T**he Failure Code**'s principles, turning challenges into opportunities and boosting your resilience and motivation.

## Embracing a POSITIVE mindset involves:

- Shifting your perception to view setbacks as learning experiences.
- Maintaining optimism to stay motivated and enthusiastic.
- Cultivating self-belief to drive determination and overcome obstacles.
- Drawing inspiration to fuel continued growth and success.

- Demonstrating tenacity to persist through challenges.
- Integrating positivity into your routine for continuous improvement.
- Keeping a clear vision to guide you through difficulties.
- Empowering yourself and others to build a supportive environment.

By incorporating these principles into your daily life, you enhance your ability to navigate obstacles and achieve success. Remember, the power of positive thinking within **The Failure Code** is not just about maintaining an optimistic outlook but about transforming challenges into opportunities and thriving in the face of adversity.

## EMBRACING CHANGE AND ADAPTABILITY

In today's fast-paced professional environment, the ability to embrace change and adapt is crucial for achieving success. Change is an inevitable part of our careers and personal development journeys, and the capacity to pivot and adjust to new circumstances can significantly impact your ability to reach your goals and overcome obstacles. As we navigate these challenges, it's essential to recognize that adaptability is not just a valuable skill but a defining factor in achieving success.

**THE FAILURE CODE** reinforces the idea that change is constant and unavoidable. Instead of resisting change, which often leads to stagnation, we should view it as an opportunity for growth and self-improvement. Embracing change allows us to uncover new strengths and capabilities and propels us toward achieving our goals. To effectively navigate this process, the framework **ADAPT** offers a strategic framework for embracing change and adaptability.

**ACCEPT CHANGE**: Embracing change starts with acceptance. Recognize that change is a natural part of life and career progression. By accepting it rather than resisting, you open yourself up to new opportunities and experiences that contribute to personal and professional growth.

**DEVELOP RESILIENCE**: Adaptability is closely tied to resilience. Develop the ability to bounce back from setbacks and challenges. Resilience helps you navigate through tough times and ensures that you remain steadfast in the face of adversity, aligning perfectly with The Failure Code's principle that setbacks are stepping stones to success.

**ALLOW FLEXIBILITY**: Flexibility is essential in adapting to new circumstances. Be willing to adjust your strategies and plans as needed. Flexibility allows you to pivot effectively and seize new opportunities, turning potential obstacles into pathways for success.

**PRIORITIZE LEARNING**: Continuous learning is a key component of adaptability. Embrace new skills and knowledge that come with change. By prioritizing learning, you equip yourself with the tools needed to handle evolving challenges and stay ahead in your career.

**TAKE INITIATIVE**: Proactively seek out and embrace change rather than waiting for it to happen. Taking initiative, positions you as a leader in managing change and enables you to shape your path rather than merely reacting to external circumstances.

## Embracing ADAPT: The Power of The Failure Code

By adopting the **ADAPT** framework, you align with **The Failure Code**'s core principles, turning change and obstacles into opportunities for growth. Embracing change with a positive mindset and proactive attitude transforms potential setbacks into stepping stones toward success.

Change is inevitable, and how you respond to it determines your ability to succeed. By being open to new experiences, developing resilience, allowing flexibility, prioritizing learning, and taking initiative, you navigate challenges with grace and determination.

Embrace change and adaptability, leverage the power of **The Failure Code**, and watch your career and personal development soar to new heights.

Let me share some real-life examples of popular personalities from sports and business who exemplified the **ADAPT** framework of **The Failure Code**:

**1. Michael Jordan**

- **ACCEPT CHANGE:** Michael Jordan initially retired from basketball in 1993 to pursue a career in baseball. Despite the change being a major shift from his successful basketball career, he accepted the challenge.
- **DEVELOP RESILIENCE**: Jordan faced numerous challenges in baseball but continued to work hard, ultimately returning to basketball with renewed vigour.
- **ALLOW FLEXIBILITY**: Upon his return, Jordan adapted his playing style to fit a more team-oriented approach, contributing to three more NBA championships with the Chicago Bulls.
- **PRIORITIZE LEARNING**: Jordan focused on improving his game and learning new skills, even after returning to basketball, refining his technique and leadership.
- **TAKE INITIATIVE**: He actively sought to improve his game and inspire his teammates, demonstrating leadership and initiative on and off the court.

## 2. Serena Williams

- **ACCEPT CHANGE**: Serena Williams has faced numerous injuries and setbacks throughout her career but has consistently accepted these changes as part of her journey.
- **DEVELOP RESILIENCE**: After each setback, including a serious health scare in 2011, Williams worked tirelessly to return to the top of the tennis world.
- **ALLOW FLEXIBILITY**: Williams has adjusted her training and

playing style to accommodate her evolving physical condition and changing dynamics in tennis.

- **PRIORITIZE LEARNING**: She continuously seeks to enhance her skills and adapt to new playing techniques and strategies.
- **TAKE INITIATIVE**: Williams proactively set goals and worked with coaches and specialists to overcome challenges and maintain her position as one of the greatest tennis players.

## 3. Elon Musk

- **ACCEPT CHANGE**: Elon Musk has embraced change by diversifying his ventures from PayPal to Tesla and SpaceX, accepting the risks associated with these new industries.
- **DEVELOP RESILIENCE**: Despite numerous setbacks, including early financial troubles and technical failures, Musk's resilience has been evident as he has persevered through challenges.
- **ALLOW FLEXIBILITY**: Musk's approach to problem-solving is highly adaptable, allowing him to pivot strategies and solutions to overcome obstacles.
- **PRIORITIZE LEARNING**: Musk prioritizes continuous learning, from understanding new technologies to acquiring knowledge in various fields relevant to his businesses.
- **TAKE INITIATIVE**: He has taken the initiative to disrupt multiple industries, pushing boundaries and driving innovation.

## 4. Howard Schultz

- **ACCEPT CHANGE**: Howard Schultz accepted the challenge of turning Starbucks from a small coffee retailer into a global brand.

- **DEVELOP RESILIENCE**: Schultz faced resistance and initial failures but remained resilient, using these experiences to refine his strategy.
- **ALLOW FLEXIBILITY**: Schultz adjusted Starbucks' business model and store formats based on customer feedback and market changes.
- **PRIORITIZE LEARNING**: He invested in learning about coffee culture and customer preferences, using this knowledge to enhance Starbucks' offerings.
- **TAKE INITIATIVE**: Schultz took bold initiatives such as expanding globally and innovating the company's menu, driving Starbucks to new heights.

## 5. Sachin Tendulkar

- **ACCEPT CHANGE**: Sachin Tendulkar faced significant challenges early in his career, including injuries and fluctuating form. He accepted these changes and continued to evolve as a player.
- **DEVELOP RESILIENCE**: Despite a few early career failures, Tendulkar demonstrated resilience by bouncing back stronger and setting numerous records in international cricket.
- **ALLOW FLEXIBILITY**: He adapted his playing style to match changing conditions and different formats of the game, such as Test cricket, One Day Internationals (ODIs), and Twenty20.
- **PRIORITIZE LEARNING**: Tendulkar continuously learned from each series and match, improving his technique and strategy to stay at the top of his game.
- **TAKE INITIATIVE**: He took the initiative to mentor younger players and contribute to Indian cricket's development, ensuring a legacy of excellence.

## 6. Narayana Murthy

- **ACCEPT CHANGE**: Narayana Murthy accepted the challenge of transforming Infosys from a small Indian IT company into a global IT services powerhouse.
- **DEVELOP RESILIENCE**: Murthy showed resilience in overcoming early business struggles and adapting to the fast-evolving technology landscape.
- **ALLOW FLEXIBILITY**: He adjusted Infosys' business model and strategies to address changing client needs and technological advancements.
- **PRIORITIZE LEARNING**: Murthy emphasized continuous learning and professional development for himself and his team, driving Infosys' success.
- **TAKE INITIATIVE**: He took the initiative to establish Infosys' unique corporate culture and governance practices, setting industry standards.

Let me share how I used this framework,

- **ACCEPT CHANGE**: I transitioned from aspiring to be a Naval Fighter Pilot to becoming a Transformation Coach, embracing a significant career shift. Accepting this change allowed me to pursue my passion in coaching and training.
- **DEVELOP RESILIENCE**: I faced numerous challenges, including starting and closing CELEB FINANCIAL PLANNERS PVT LTD. Despite these setbacks, I demonstrated resilience by refocusing my career on training and coaching, ultimately achieving success.
- **ALLOW FLEXIBILITY**: In my journey, I adapted to different roles, from Sales Officer to Life Skills Facilitator and Leadership Trainer. My flexibility in shifting career paths and learning new skills has been crucial in my success.
- **PRIORITIZE LEARNING**: I continually invest in personal development and learning, staying updated with industry

trends and methodologies. This commitment has helped ME create effective training programs and content.

- **TAKE INITIATIVE**: I have taken the initiative in designing and delivering impactful training programs, writing books, and creating YouTube content. My proactive approach has allowed me to make a significant impact in the field of professional development.
- By applying the **ADAPT** framework, so many people including me have demonstrated how embracing change, developing resilience, allowing flexibility, prioritizing learning, and taking initiative can lead to success and growth.

■■

## HARNESSING SELF-CONFIDENCE AND SELF-BELIEF

Harnessing self-confidence and self-belief is a cornerstone of the success formula outlined in **The Failure Code**. In the fast-paced and often challenging world of working professionals, cultivating a strong sense of self-assurance is crucial for overcoming obstacles and achieving our goals. When we believe in ourselves and our capabilities, we unlock our full potential and open doors to new opportunities for growth and success.

Self-confidence is not a trait we are born with; it is a skill that can be developed and strengthened over time. One effective way to build self-confidence is by setting and achieving small, realistic goals. Celebrating these accomplishments, no matter how minor they may seem, creates a positive feedback loop that reinforces our belief in our abilities. This gradual build-up of confidence prepares us for more significant challenges and achievements.

Similarly, self-belief is closely tied to self-confidence and involves having unwavering faith in our potential to succeed. When we trust in our own abilities, we are more inclined to take calculated risks, step out of our comfort zones, and persevere despite difficulties.

Cultivating a mindset of self-belief empowers us to overcome obstacles and emerge stronger and more resilient.

**The Failure Code** teaches us that failure is not a dead end but a stepping stone on the path to success. By harnessing our self-confidence and self-belief, we can learn from setbacks, adapt our strategies, and continue progressing towards our goals. With a positive mindset and unwavering faith in ourselves, no challenge is too great to overcome.

To effectively harness self-confidence and self-belief, we can use the **SELF-BELIEF** framework:

- **SET ACHIEVABLE GOALS**: Establish small, manageable goals and celebrate each success to build confidence progressively.
- **EDUCATE YOURSELF**: Continuously learn and grow to enhance your skills and knowledge, reinforcing your self-assurance.
- **LEVERAGE STRENGTHS**: Focus on and utilize your strengths to boost confidence and tackle challenges more effectively.
- **FOSTER POSITIVE MINDSET**: Maintain a positive attitude, even in the face of setbacks, to keep self-belief strong.
- **BELIEVE IN YOUR POTENTIAL**: Cultivate an unwavering faith in your ability to succeed, which will drive you to take risks and persevere.
- **EMBRACE FAILURE AS LEARNING**: View failures as opportunities to learn and improve, rather than as deterrents.
- **LEAD WITH CONFIDENCE**: Approach challenges with self-assurance and conviction, inspiring confidence in others as well.
- **INVEST IN PERSONAL GROWTH**: Continuously invest in your personal and professional development to maintain and enhance self-belief.

- **EXERCISE RESILIENCE**: Develop the ability to bounce back from setbacks, reinforcing your confidence and determination.
- **FOCUS ON ACHIEVEMENTS**: Regularly remind yourself of your accomplishments and progress to sustain a positive self-view.

By integrating the **SELF-BELIEF** framework from **The Failure Code** into your professional and personal life, you can effectively harness self-confidence and self-belief. This will enable you to face challenges with greater resilience, adapt strategies as needed, and advance towards your goals with unwavering determination.

Remember, the power to succeed lies within you. Embrace the principles of **The Failure Code**, cultivate a positive mindset, and let your self-confidence and self-belief guide you to achieve greatness.

## Let me share with you a Real-Life Case Study: Boosting Self-Confidence with the SELF-BELIEF Framework

This is about one of my clients who I was coaching.

He is a seasoned sales professional working in a company providing architecture services to the real estate industry, with 10 years of experience but struggling with low self-belief.

**Objective:** To help the client develop self-confidence and overcome his low self-belief issue.

## Application of the SELF-BELIEF Framework:

1. **S SET ACHIEVABLE GOALS:**
   - **Action:** We started by setting small, achievable sales targets for him. Instead of focusing on large, intimidating goals, we broke them down into manageable milestones.
   - **Outcome:** By consistently hitting these smaller targets, he

experienced regular successes that helped build his confidence gradually.

2. **E-EDUCATE YOURSELF:**

- **Action:** I encouraged him to invest time in learning more about the latest trends and innovations in the architecture and real estate industry. We arranged for him to attend webinars and workshops.
- **Outcome:** Enhanced knowledge and skills made him feel more competent and better prepared to engage with clients, which bolstered his self-assurance.

3. **L-LEVERAGE STRENGTHS:**

- **Action:** We identified his core strengths, such as his deep industry knowledge and strong client relationship skills. We focused on leveraging these strengths in his sales approach.
- **Outcome:** By capitalizing on his strengths, he felt more confident in his abilities and saw positive results in his interactions with clients.

4. **F-FOSTER POSITIVE MINDSET:**

- **Action:** We worked on cultivating a positive mindset through daily affirmations and positive self-talk. We also practiced reframing negative thoughts into positive ones.
- **Outcome:** This shift in mindset helped him approach challenges with a more optimistic attitude, reducing his self-doubt.

5. **B-BELIEVE IN YOUR POTENTIAL:**

- **Action:** We focused on reinforcing his belief in his potential by reviewing his past successes and achievements. We discussed how his experience and expertise were valuable assets.
- **Outcome:** Reaffirming his potential helped him regain confidence and encouraged him to take on more

challenging projects.

6. **E-EMBRACE FAILURE AS LEARNING:**

- **Action:** I guided him to view setbacks not as failures but as opportunities to learn and grow. We analyzed past unsuccessful sales attempts to extract lessons and improve future strategies.
- **Outcome:** Viewing failures as learning experiences reduced his fear of making mistakes and improved his resilience.

7. **L-LEAD WITH CONFIDENCE:**

- **Action:** We practiced scenarios where he needed to assert himself in client meetings and presentations. I provided feedback and encouragement to help him present with confidence.
- **Outcome:** Improved presentation skills and assertiveness led to better client interactions and increased confidence.

8. **I-INVEST IN PERSONAL GROWTH:**

- **Action:** I recommended that he continue investing in his personal development by pursuing relevant certifications and training.
- **Outcome:** Continued growth and learning kept him engaged and motivated, further enhancing his self-confidence.

9. **E-EXERCISE RESILIENCE:**

- **Action:** We focused on building his resilience by setting up strategies to manage stress and setbacks effectively. We developed a plan to handle difficult situations and bounce back quickly.
- **Outcome:** Increased resilience allowed him to handle challenges more effectively and maintain his confidence during tough times.

10. **F-FOCUS ON ACHIEVEMENTS:**

- **Action:** We regularly reviewed and celebrated his achievements, no matter how small. We maintained a record of successes to track progress.
- **Outcome:** Recognizing and celebrating achievements kept his self-belief strong and reminded him of his capabilities.

■■■

# CHAPTER 5

## STAY MOTIVATED IN THE PURSUIT OF SUCCESS

# FINDING YOUR WHY

In this sub-chapter, **"Finding Your Why"**, we will delve into the foundational principle of success—understanding your purpose and motivation in life. As working professionals, having a clear sense of **why** you do what you do every day is crucial. Without this sense of purpose, it's easy to become lost in the daily grind and lose sight of your long-term goals.

**The Failure Code** offers a unique perspective on success, emphasizing the importance of aligning your actions with your values and passions. **Finding your why** is about tapping into a deep reservoir of motivation that propels you to overcome obstacles and persist through challenges in your career, personal life, or relationships.

## Finding Your Why: The WHY Framework

### 1. WHAT DRIVES YOU?

- **Action:** Reflect on what excites and motivates you. Identify activities, causes, or values that resonate deeply with you.
- **Example:** A sales professional may discover a passion for helping clients achieve their goals, which drives their enthusiasm and performance.

### 2. HISTORICAL INSIGHTS

- **Action:** Analyse past experiences to uncover patterns or moments that have significantly impacted you. Look for recurring themes in your achievements and setbacks.
- **Example:** A project manager might realize that their greatest satisfaction comes from leading teams through challenging projects, revealing a passion for leadership and problem-solving.

**3. YOUR CORE VALUES**

- **Action:** Identify your core values and principles. Determine how they align with your daily activities and long-term aspirations.
- **Example:** An entrepreneur might value innovation and creativity, leading them to pursue ventures that align with these values, fueling their commitment and persistence.

**4. IMAGINE YOUR IDEAL FUTURE**

- **Action:** Visualize where you see yourself in the future. Envision your ideal career, life, or relationships, and connect this vision with your current efforts.
- **Example:** A teacher might imagine a future where they have positively impacted thousands of students, motivating them to continuously improve their teaching methods.

**5. Transform Your Vision into Goals**

- **Action:** Translate your vision and purpose into actionable goals. Set clear, achievable objectives that align with your why.
- **Example:** A writer may set goals to complete a book and share their insights with the world, driven by their passion for storytelling and knowledge-sharing.

**6. VALUE YOUR PROGRESS**

- **Action:** Regularly assess your progress towards your goals and how well they align with your why. Celebrate achievements and make adjustments as needed.
- **Example:** An athlete might track their progress in training and competition, celebrating milestones that bring them closer to their vision of success.

**7. ENGAGE WITH YOUR SUPPORT NETWORK**

- **Action:** Share your why with mentors, colleagues, and loved ones. Seek their support and feedback to stay motivated and aligned with your purpose.

- **Example:** A start-up founder might engage with advisors and a supportive community to gain encouragement and practical advice on their entrepreneurial journey.

<u>**8. REVIEW AND REFLECT**</u>

- **Action:** Periodically review and reflect on your why. Ensure that your actions and goals remain aligned with your evolving purpose and values.
- **Example:** A career professional might reassess their goals and motivations every few years to ensure they continue to align with their personal growth and career aspirations.

## Application of the WHY Framework:

### My Journey

During my career, I applied the **WHY** framework to align my professional efforts with my core values and long-term aspirations. Early on, I recognized that my passion for transforming lives through coaching and training was central to my purpose. Here's how the **WHY** framework guided me:

- **What Drives You?**
  - My drive was fueled by a deep desire to help individuals unlock their potential and achieve their goals. This realization guided my decision to focus on life skills and leadership training.
- **Historical Insights**
  - Reflecting on my past experiences, I identified a pattern of satisfaction derived from facilitating personal and professional growth in others, shaping my career focus.
- **Your Core Values**
  - I aligned my work with values such as empathy, growth, and resilience, ensuring that my efforts were meaningful and consistent with my beliefs.

- **Imagine Your Ideal Future**
    - I envisioned a future where I could make a significant impact through my training programs and coaching, motivating me to pursue this path with dedication.
- **Transform Your Vision into Goals**
    - I set specific goals to develop and deliver impactful training programs, author books, and provide coaching that aligns with my vision of empowering others.
- **Value Your Progress**
    - I celebrated milestones such as successful workshops and positive feedback from clients, using these achievements to fuel further growth and improvement.
- **Engage with Your Support Network**
    - I engaged with mentors and peers in the coaching community to gain insights and support, which helped me refine my approach and stay aligned with my purpose.
- **Review and Reflect**
    - Periodically, I reviewed my goals and the impact of my work to ensure they continued to align with my evolving purpose and personal growth.

By finding and embracing my why, I transformed challenges into opportunities for growth and maintained a clear direction in my career. The **WHY** framework not only helped me stay motivated but also guided me towards achieving meaningful success.

Remember, understanding your why is the fuel that drives you toward greatness. Take the time to discover it, align your actions with it, and let it guide you on your journey to success.

■■

# CREATING A VISION BOARD FOR INSPIRATION

In this sub-chapter, **"Creating a Vision Board for Inspiration,"** we will explore how to harness the power of visualization to stay motivated and focused on your goals using a vision board. This concept ties closely with **The Failure Code**, a success formula that emphasizes personal development, resilience, and a positive mindset.

## What is a Vision Board?

A **vision board** is a visual representation of your goals, dreams, and aspirations. It typically consists of a collage of images, words, and phrases that symbolize what you want to achieve. By creating a vision board, you make your goals more tangible and vivid, reinforcing your commitment to achieving them.

## How to Create a Vision Board?

1. **Define Your Goals and Aspirations**
    - **Action:** Start by identifying your short-term and long-term goals. Consider various aspects of your life, including career, personal development, relationships, and health.
    - **Example:** If your goal is to advance in your career, you might include images of leadership positions or successful projects.
2. **Gather Materials**
    - **Action:** Collect magazines, printouts, quotes, and other materials that resonate with your goals. You'll also need a board (corkboard, poster board, or digital tool) and adhesive materials.
    - **Example:** You might find inspirational quotes about leadership or images of your desired work environment.
3. **Create Your Vision Board**
    - **Action:** Arrange the collected materials on your board in a

visually appealing way. Organize them to represent different areas of your life and goals.

- **Example:** Position career-related images at the center and personal goals along the edges to maintain focus on your primary objectives.

4. **Display Your Vision Board**

- **Action:** Place your vision board in a prominent location where you will see it daily. This constant visual reminder will keep your goals top of mind.
- **Example:** Position your vision board near your workspace or bedroom to stay motivated throughout the day.

5. **Engage with Your Vision Board Regularly**

- **Action:** Spend a few minutes each day visualizing your success and reflecting on the images and words on your board. Adjust the board as needed to align with evolving goals.
- **Example:** Take a moment each morning to envision achieving the goals depicted on your board, reinforcing your commitment.

## How to Implement Your Vision Board in Your Life?

1. **Stay Motivated and Focused**

- **Action:** Use your vision board as a source of motivation during challenging times. Let it remind you of your goals and the reasons behind them.
- **Example:** When facing setbacks, glance at your vision board to renew your focus and motivation.

2. **Reinforce Positive Affirmations**

- **Action:** Incorporate positive affirmations and success statements into your vision board. This helps in reinforcing a positive mindset.

- **Example:** Add affirmations like "I am capable of achieving my goals" to boost your confidence and resilience.

3. **Celebrate Progress**

   - **Action:** Acknowledge and celebrate milestones achieved towards your goals. Update your vision board to reflect new goals and aspirations.
   - **Example:** Once you accomplish a goal, replace or add new images and words that represent your next set of aspirations.

## Vision Board and The Failure Code

The vision board is an integral part of **The Failure Code**, which emphasizes personal development, resilience, and a positive mindset. Here's how it aligns with the code:

- **Personal Development:** Creating a vision board is an active step in personal growth. It helps clarify your goals and aspirations, providing a clear direction for your development.
- **Resilience:** A vision board serves as a daily reminder of your goals, helping you stay resilient and focused even when faced with challenges and setbacks.
- **Positive Mindset:** By regularly engaging with your vision board, you reinforce positive affirmations and maintain a hopeful outlook, which is crucial for overcoming obstacles.

## How I have used Vision Boards to achieve success in life?

In my own journey, I have utilized vision boards to stay aligned with my goals and aspirations. For example, when transitioning from a career in sales to becoming a life skills trainer, I created a vision board that included images of successful training sessions, inspirational quotes, and milestones I wanted to achieve.

1. **Defining Goals:**
    - I set clear goals related to my new career path, such as conducting workshops and authoring books.
2. **Gathering Materials:**
    - I collected images of training sessions, motivational quotes, and symbols of personal growth.
3. **Creating the Board:**
    - I arranged these materials on a board, ensuring it reflected my new career aspirations and personal development goals.
4. **Displaying and Engaging:**
    - I placed the board in my office, making it a daily source of inspiration and motivation.
5. **Celebrating Progress:**
    - As I achieved milestones, I updated my board to reflect new goals and continue my journey of growth.

By creating and using a vision board, I was able to maintain a clear focus on my goals, stay motivated, and navigate challenges effectively. This tool has been instrumental in aligning my actions with my aspirations and driving my success.

So, take some time to create your own vision board, and watch how it transforms your approach to achieving success. With a clear visual representation of your goals, you'll find renewed motivation and a more focused path to success.

■■

# SURROUNDING YOURSELF WITH POSITIVE INFLUENCES

In the pursuit of success, one of the most impactful strategies is to surround yourself with positive influences. These influences can come from various sources—supportive friends, encouraging family members, inspirational books, and motivational podcasts. The idea is that your environment significantly shapes your mindset, motivation, and ultimately, your success.

## The Power of Positive Influences

The principle behind surrounding yourself with positive influences is rooted in the belief that **"You are the average of the five people you spend the most time with."** This powerful quote highlights how your close circle has a profound effect on your behaviour, attitudes, and success. The people you interact with regularly set the tone for your mindset and performance, making it essential to choose those who uplift and inspire you.

### The Role of Positive Influences in The Failure Code

**The Failure Code** emphasizes that success is not achieved in isolation but through the collaborative support and encouragement from others. Here's how surrounding yourself with positive influences aligns with the principles of **The Failure Code**:

- **Support System:** Positive influences provide you with encouragement and guidance, helping you navigate challenges and maintain a growth-oriented mindset. When surrounded by individuals who believe in your potential, you're more likely to persevere and achieve your goals.
- **Inspiration and Motivation:** Positive influences offer inspiration and motivation, which are crucial for overcoming obstacles. When you engage with uplifting and motivating sources, you boost your resilience and determination to push through setbacks.

- **Personal Growth:** Being in a positive environment fosters personal development. When you interact with people who push you to be your best self, you're more likely to grow, evolve, and reach your full potential.

## Thought Model: The Influence of Positive Networks

**The Social Learning Theory**, developed by Albert Bandura, provides a valuable framework for understanding the power of positive influences. This theory suggests that people learn behaviours, attitudes, and emotional reactions through observation and interaction with others. Here's how it applies to surrounding yourself with positive influences:

1. **OBSERVATION:** You observe the behaviours and attitudes of those around you. If your circle exhibits positivity, resilience, and success-oriented behaviours, you are more likely to adopt similar traits.
2. **IMITATION:** You emulate the actions and attitudes of those you spend the most time with. Being around positive influences encourages you to mirror their optimism, work ethic, and approach to challenges.
3. **REINFORCEMENT:** Positive feedback and encouragement from your network reinforce your own positive behaviours and attitudes. When your efforts are supported and recognized, you're motivated to continue striving towards your goals.

## How to Cultivate Positive Influences

1. **IDENTIFY YOUR CIRCLE**

- **Action:** Reflect on the five people you spend the most time with. Evaluate how they influence your mindset and goals.
- **Example:** If your current circle includes individuals who are pessimistic or unsupportive, consider expanding your

network to include more positive influences.

2. **SEEK OUT UPLIFTING RELATIONSHIPS**
    - **Action:** Build connections with people who inspire, motivate, and support you. Look for mentors, colleagues, or friends who share your values and ambitions.
    - **Example:** Join professional groups, attend networking events, or engage with online communities that align with your goals.
3. **ENGAGE WITH INSPIRATIONAL CONTENT**
    - **Action:** Incorporate motivational books, podcasts, and seminars into your routine. These resources can provide additional positive reinforcement and guidance.
    - **Example:** Follow thought leaders in your field and consume content that aligns with your goals and aspirations.
4. **FOSTER POSITIVE INTERACTIONS**
    - **Action:** Cultivate and maintain supportive and constructive relationships. Be proactive in offering support and encouragement to others as well.
    - **Example:** Regularly check in with your mentors or colleagues, and celebrate each other's successes.

## My Approach to Positive Influences: How I used this to my success

In my own journey, I have embraced the power of surrounding myself with positive influences. By consciously choosing mentors, colleagues, and friends who uplift and inspire me, I have created a supportive network that has significantly contributed to my success.

1. **EVALUATING MY CIRCLE:**
    - I regularly assess the impact of my close relationships on my goals and mindset.

2. **SEEKING UPLIFTING RELATIONSHIPS:**

- I actively seek connections with individuals who share my values and drive.

3. **ENGAGING WITH INSPIRATIONAL CONTENT:**

- I incorporate books, podcasts, and seminars into my routine to stay motivated and informed.

4. **FOSTERING POSITIVE INTERACTIONS:**

- I maintain strong, supportive relationships and provide encouragement to those in my network.

By surrounding myself with positive influences, I have been able to navigate challenges with resilience and stay focused on my goals. This approach has played a crucial role in my personal and professional development.

## Let us see how Sundar Pichai used this to his benefit:

**Sundar Pichai**, the CEO of Alphabet Inc. and Google LLC, is a prominent example of how surrounding oneself with positive influences can lead to extraordinary success. Pichai's journey is a testament to the power of a supportive network and inspirational mentors.

**1. EARLY CAREER AND EDUCATION**

Pichai was born in Madurai, India, and completed his engineering degree at the Indian Institute of Technology (IIT) Kharagpur. His initial success was fueled by the encouragement and support from his family and mentors at IIT Kharagpur. The rigorous academic environment and the guidance he received there played a significant role in shaping his career aspirations.

**2. JOINING GOOGLE**

When Pichai joined Google in 2004, he was mentored by some of the brightest minds in the tech industry. The culture at Google, known for its innovation and collaborative spirit, provided him with a positive and growth-oriented environment. His work on the Google Toolbar and Google Chrome was supported by influential leaders within the company, which significantly contributed to his professional growth.

**3. PROMOTION TO CEO**

Pichai's rise to CEO in 2015 was a result of his ability to navigate the corporate world with the support of positive influences. He was mentored by Google's co-founders Larry Page and Sergey Brin, as well as other key leaders in the tech industry. Their belief in his capabilities and their constructive feedback were crucial in shaping his leadership style and strategic vision.

**4. BUILDING A SUPPORTIVE NETWORK**

Pichai has often spoken about the importance of having a supportive network. His positive relationships with colleagues and mentors have been instrumental in his journey. He actively engages with his team, fosters a culture of collaboration, and values the input and encouragement from those around him.

**5. IMPACT OF POSITIVE INFLUENCES**

Under Pichai's leadership, Google has continued to thrive and innovate, with numerous successful projects and a positive work culture. His ability to surround himself with positive, forward-thinking individuals has been a key factor in his success.

## How Sundar Pichai's Example Relates to Surrounding Yourself with Positive Influences

1. **SUPPORT SYSTEM:**

- Pichai's early support from family, mentors, and colleagues helped him navigate his career path and overcome challenges.

2. **INSPIRATION AND MOTIVATION:**

- The encouragement from influential figures at Google

provided him with the motivation to excel and drive innovation.

3. **PERSONAL GROWTH:**
   - Positive feedback and a supportive work environment at Google contributed to Pichai's personal and professional development.
4. **RESILIENCE:**
   - The guidance and positive reinforcement from his network enabled him to handle setbacks and continue pushing towards his goals.

Sundar Pichai's career demonstrates the profound impact of surrounding oneself with positive influences. By leveraging support, inspiration, and constructive feedback from his network, he has achieved remarkable success and continues to inspire others in the tech industry. His story underscores the importance of cultivating a supportive environment to achieve personal and professional goals.

■■■

# CHAPTER 6

## APPLYING THE FAILURE CODE TO YOUR PROFESSIONAL LIFE

# IMPLEMENTING THE FAILURE CODE IN YOUR CAREER

Congratulations on taking the first step towards unlocking your full potential by diving into cracking **The Failure Code,** a success formula that never fails.

In this chapter we will discuss how you can implement **The Failure Code** in your career to achieve greater success and fulfilment.

**THE FAILURE CODE** is not just a set of guidelines or principles; it is a mindset that, when embraced whole heartedly can transform your career and your life.

The understanding that failure is not the end but rather a stepping stone towards success, you can approach challenges with a sense of resilience and determination.

One of the key aspects of implementing **The Failure Code** in your career is to view obstacles not as roadblocks but as opportunities for growth and learning. When faced with setbacks or challenges remember the they are not a reflection of your ability but rather a chance to refine your skills and develop a stronger mindset.

Another important factor to consider when implementing **The Failure Code** in your career is to maintain a positive attitude and mindset. By focusing on the lessons learnt from failure rather than dwelling on the negative aspects you can cultivate a sense of optimism and motivation that will propel you towards your goals.

Finally, remember that success is not a destination but a journey.

By embracing **The Failure Code** and viewing failure as a necessary part of growth, you can navigate the ups and downs of your career with grace and resilience.

With the right mindset and determination, you can overcome any obstacle and achieve the success you truly deserve.

So as you a embark on this journey of self-discovery and personal development, remember that failure is not the end but merely a stepping stone towards your ultimate success.

Embrace **The Failure Code**, cultivate opposite mind set, and watch as your career flourishes beyond your wildest dreams.

■■■

# CHAPTER 7

## STORY OF A MAN CALLED FAILURE

## CHAPTER 1: THE DESPONDENT MENTOR

In a small town lived a man named FAILURE. Despite being one of the town's first settlers, FAILURE was not known for his wisdom or encouragement. His name seemed to define his outlook on life: pessimistic, reality-avoiding, and devoid of support for those around him.

FAILURE was a recluse, always shying away from facing reality and acknowledging his setbacks. When people in the town encountered difficulties and approached FAILURE for guidance, he would only shrug and say, "What's the point? It's all doomed anyway."

One day, a young woman named HOPE came to FAILURE. She had just lost her job and felt utterly defeated. "Can you help me, FAILURE?" she asked, her voice trembling.

FAILURE sighed deeply, "Why bother trying? It's probably just going to happen again. Just accept it and move on."

Hope left feeling worse than before, her spirit crushed by FAILURE's bleak outlook. The town had had enough.

They decided to hold a meeting to address FAILURE's attitude. One of the elders in the town, Wisdom, popularly known as CODE, spoke first, "FAILURE, your name does not have to define you negatively. You have the potential to be a great mentor if you change your perspective."

## CHAPTER 2: THE TURNING POINT

FAILURE scoffed, "How can I be anything more than what I am? I've only ever seen failure."

Wisdom looked at him kindly, "Every failure is a lesson in disguise. It's time you learn from your own experiences and help others do the same. I will give you a formula, also named FAILURE. You practice that."

Reluctantly, FAILURE agreed to try the formula given by Wisdom. He started by facing his own past, reflecting on the times he had given up too easily and the missed opportunities for growth.

## CHAPTER 3: THE HONEST REALIZATION

FAILURE began to be honest with himself. He faced the reality that his negative attitude had not only hindered his own progress but also the progress of those who sought his help. He acknowledged his role in spreading hopelessness and resolved to change.

When Hope returned, FAILURE greeted her differently this time. "I'm sorry for my previous advice," he said. "Let's face this together and see what we can learn from it."

## CHAPTER 4: THE ANALYTICAL BREAKDOWN

FAILURE sat with Hope and analyzed her situation. They broke down the reasons she lost her job and identified areas for improvement. FAILURE realized that by understanding the root causes, they could develop strategies to avoid similar pitfalls in the future.

Hope left their meeting with a newfound sense of direction and determination.

## CHAPTER 5: THE EMPATHETIC SHIFT

FAILURE began to understand the emotional impact of his words. He started listening more and offering support. When people came to him, he would say, "I understand how you feel. Let's work through this together."

People in the town started to feel a change. FAILURE was no longer a source of despair but a beacon of empathy and support.

## CHAPTER 6: THE INNOVATIVE APPROACH

FAILURE started seeing setbacks as opportunities for innovation. He encouraged people to think outside the box and find creative solutions to their problems. He shared stories of inventors and leaders who had turned their failures into stepping stones for success.

## CHAPTER 7: THE OPTIMISTIC PERSPECTIVE

FAILURE adopted an optimistic view, seeing every failure as a temporary setback. He began telling people, "This is not the end. It's just a part of the journey. There are better things ahead." He helped the townspeople see that failure was not final but a crucial part of the path to success.

## CHAPTER 8: THE CELEBRATORY ATTITUDE

FAILURE found joy in the journey. He started celebrating small victories and progress, no matter how insignificant they seemed. "Every step forward is a reason to celebrate," he would say. The town began to thrive with this new energy, finding happiness even in their struggles.

## CHAPTER 9: THE EXPERIENCED GUIDE

FAILURE used his past experiences to build resilience in others. He shared his own stories of transformation and the lessons he had learned. "I've been there," he would say, "and I know you can come out stronger."

## EPILOGUE: THE TRANSFORMED MENTOR

FAILURE had truly transformed. No longer a symbol of defeat, he became a mentor who embodied honesty, analytical thinking, empathy, innovation, optimism, celebration, and experience.

Hope, now thriving in her new job, looked back at her journey and smiled. "Thank you, FAILURE," she said one day. "You've shown me that failure is not the end, but the beginning of something greater."

FAILURE nodded, a warm smile on his face. "And thank you, Hope, for showing me that change is always possible."

From that day forward, FAILURE continued to guide the townspeople, helping them turn their setbacks into successes, and proving that even the darkest times can lead to the brightest transformations.

But this transformation was not possible without Wisdom, aka CODE, who was a seasoned coach.

**Let us draw parallels between FAILURE and Sundar Pichai**

Sundar Pichai, the CEO of Alphabet Inc. and Google LLC, is a prime example of this transformation in real life. Despite the setbacks and challenges, his journey reflects how surrounding oneself with positive influences and mentors can lead to extraordinary success. Pichai's story, much like FAILURE's transformation, underscores the importance of a supportive network and the power of resilience and optimism.

■■■

# CHAPTER 8

## THE COACH CALLED CODE

## CODE- THE COACH

CODE was a seasoned coach known for transforming setbacks into comebacks. With a structured and empathetic approach, CODE used to guide individuals to unlock their potential and navigate through their failures.

**CODE - The Coaching Philosophy**

CODE's coaching philosophy was built on four pillars:

**C**- Clarity

**O**-Ownership

**D**-Development

**E**-Empowerment

■■

## 4 PILLAR CODE COACHING SYSTEM

C - **Clarity:** Gain clear understanding and insight into the situation.

**Action:** Help clients like FAILURE to clearly define their goals, identify the root causes of their setbacks, and understand the context of their failures. This includes honest self-reflection and the separation of facts from emotions.

**Example:** CODE asks FAILURE to list specific instances of failure and break down the contributing factors. They work together to identify patterns and clarify what FAILURE truly wants to achieve.

■■

**O - Ownership:** Take responsibility and control over actions and outcomes.

**Action:** Encourage clients to accept responsibility for their actions without self-blame. This involves understanding their role in the outcome and recognizing the power they have to change future results.

**Example:** CODE helps FAILURE to acknowledge his role in past failures without dwelling on guilt. They create a plan where FAILURE takes proactive steps toward improvement and owns his progress.

■■

**D - Development:** Focus on continuous learning and skill-building.

**Action:** Create a personalized development plan that includes setting realistic goals, acquiring new skills, and learning from each experience. Emphasize the importance of growth mindset and resilience.

**Example:** CODE and FAILURE set specific, measurable goals for personal and professional growth. They identify resources and opportunities for learning, such as workshops, courses, or mentorship programs.

■■

**E - Empowerment:** Build confidence and enable self-efficacy.

**Action:** Empower clients to take initiative, make decisions, and believe in their ability to succeed. Foster a supportive environment that encourages risk-taking and celebrates achievements.

**Example:** CODE provides FAILURE with tools and techniques to boost his confidence, such as positive affirmations, visualization, and incremental challenges. They celebrate small victories to reinforce FAILURE's sense of accomplishment.

■■

# HOW CODE COACHED FAILURE?

FAILURE had been struggling with his pessimistic outlook and lack of progress. Hearing about CODE's reputation as a transformative coach, FAILURE decided to seek help.

## SEEKING CLARITY

FAILURE met with CODE, who began by helping him gain clarity. They sat down and meticulously went through FAILURE's past experiences. CODE asked probing questions, helping FAILURE to see patterns and understand the root causes of his setbacks. By separating emotions from facts, FAILURE began to see his situation with a clearer perspective.

## Embracing Ownership

With a newfound clarity, CODE guided FAILURE towards ownership. They discussed the importance of taking responsibility for one's actions. CODE helped FAILURE understand that while external factors could contribute to failure, his responses and actions were within his control. This realization was empowering, as FAILURE began to feel a sense of agency over his life.

## FOCUSING ON DEVELOPMENT

Next CODE and FAILURE crafted a development plan. They set specific, achievable goals for both personal growth and skill enhancement. CODE encouraged FAILURE to enroll in courses and seek mentorship opportunities. They worked on building a growth mindset, emphasizing that each failure was a stepping stone towards improvement. FAILURE started to see setbacks as valuable learning experiences.

## FINDING EMPOWERMENT

Finally, CODE focused on empowering FAILURE. They worked on building FAILURE's confidence through various techniques like positive affirmations and visualization. CODE challenged FAILURE with incremental tasks that pushed him out of his comfort zone but were achievable. Each small victory was celebrated, reinforcing FAILURE's belief in his capabilities.

**The Framework he used to help FAILURE was also named as FAILURE, and ever since then it became the popular FAILURE FRAMEWORK for SUCCESS.**

■■■

# CHAPTER 9

# THE

# F.A.I.L.U.R.E

# FRAMEWORK

## F.A.I.L.U.R.E. FRAMEWORK

**1. F - Face the Reality**

- Concept: Accept the failure without denial. Acknowledge it as part of the journey.
- Action: Reflect on what went wrong without making excuses. Understand that failure is a natural part of growth.

**2. A - Analyze the Situation**

- Concept: Break down the failure to extract valuable lessons.
- Action: Identify the root causes and specific mistakes. Document what you have learned and how you can avoid similar issues in the future.

**3. I - Integrate Emotional Management**

- Concept: Manage the emotional impact of failure.
- Action: Practice self-care and seek support from friends, mentors, or professionals. Embrace activities that help you process and release negative emotions.

**4. L - Leverage the Learning**

- Concept: Use failure as a stepping stone to success.
- Action: Apply the lessons learned to future endeavours. Adjust strategies and plans based on insights gained from the failure.

**5. U - Understand the Outcome**

- Concept: View failure as an outcome, not a final destination.
- Action: Reframe failure as feedback rather than a verdict on your abilities. Recognize that every setback is an opportunity for a comeback.

6. **R - Rejoice in the Journey**

- **Concept: Celebrate failure as a blessing in disguise.**
- **Action: Appreciate the growth and resilience developed through failure. Share your story and the insights gained to inspire others.**

7. **E - Experience and Evolve**

- **Concept: Embrace failure as a valuable experience.**
- **Action: Focus on continuous improvement and resilience. Understand that each failure contributes to your overall development and prepares you for future challenges.**

### How I Implemented the FAILURE Framework in My Life

Throughout my journey, I've encountered numerous setbacks and challenges. However, by implementing the FAILURE Framework, I transformed these obstacles into stepping stones toward success. Here's how each element of the framework played a pivotal role in my personal and professional growth:

### F - Face the Reality

Concept: Accept the failure without denial. Acknowledge it as part of the journey.

Action: Reflect on what went wrong without making excuses. Understand that failure is a natural part of growth.

## My Experience:

Facing the reality of my failures was the hardest part. When my venture, CELEB FINANCIAL PLANNERS PVT LTD, shut down after 2.5 years, I was devastated. Instead of making excuses, I sat down and reflected on what went wrong. I accepted that failure is a natural part of any journey and that acknowledging it was the first step towards growth.

### A - Analyze the Situation

Concept: Break down the failure to extract valuable lessons.

Action: Identify the root causes and specific mistakes. Document what you have learned and how you can avoid similar issues in the future.

## My Experience:

I analyzed every aspect of my failed venture. I identified the root causes, such as poor market research and inadequate financial planning. I documented these lessons and used them to avoid similar mistakes in the future. This analysis became a foundation for my subsequent successes in sales and training.

### I - Integrate Emotional Management

Concept: Manage the emotional impact of failure.

Action: Practice self-care and seek support from friends, mentors, or professionals. Embrace activities that help you process and release negative emotions.

## My Experience:

The emotional toll of failure can be overwhelming. I started practicing self-care by engaging in activities that brought me peace, such as meditation and exercise. I also sought support from mentors who provided valuable guidance. Managing my emotions helped me stay focused and resilient during tough times.

### L - Leverage the Learning

Concept: Use failure as a stepping stone to success.

Action: Apply the lessons learned to future endeavors. Adjust strategies and plans based on insights gained from the failure.

## My Experience:

I applied the lessons from my failed venture to my future endeavors. When I transitioned into training and coaching, I used the insights gained to refine my strategies. This approach helped me build a successful career, impacting countless individuals through my training programs.

### U - Understand the Outcome

Concept: View failure as an outcome, not a final destination.

Action: Reframe failure as feedback rather than a verdict on your abilities. Recognize that every setback is an opportunity for a comeback.

## My Experience:

I started viewing failure as valuable feedback. Each setback was not a final destination but an opportunity for a comeback. This mindset shift allowed me to approach challenges with renewed energy and optimism, knowing that each failure brought me closer to success.

### R - Rejoice in the Journey

Concept: Celebrate failure as a blessing in disguise.

Action: Appreciate the growth and resilience developed through failure. Share your story and the insights gained to inspire others.

## My Experience:

I began celebrating the journey, including the failures. Each failure taught me resilience and growth. I shared my story with others, inspiring them to see failure as a blessing in disguise. This celebration of the journey kept me motivated and focused on continuous improvement.

### E - Experience and Evolve

Concept: Embrace failure as a valuable experience.

Action: Focus on continuous improvement and resilience. Understand that each failure contributes to your overall development and prepares you for future challenges.

## My Experience:

I embraced failure as a valuable experience. Each failure contributed to my development, preparing me for future challenges. By focusing on continuous improvement and resilience,

I evolved into a more effective and impactful trainer and coach.

# Epilogue

## The Transformed Professional

Through the FAILURE Framework, I transformed my setbacks into successes. This journey taught me that failure is not the end but a crucial part of growth and achievement. By facing reality, analyzing situations, managing emotions, leveraging learnings, understanding outcomes, rejoicing in the journey, and evolving through experiences, I became a more resilient and successful professional.

Remember, failure is not a verdict but a vital component of the path to success. Embrace it, learn from it, and let it propel you towards your goals.

■■■

# CHAPTER 10

## THE SUCCESS STORIES

# SUCCESS STORIES OF PROFESSIONALS WHO CRACKED THE FAILURE CODE

In this subchapter, we will delve into the inspiring stories of professionals who have managed to crack the failure code and emerge victorious in their careers. These individuals serve as shining examples of resilience, determination, and unwavering belief in their abilities.

By studying their journeys, we can glean valuable insights and strategies to overcome our own obstacles and achieve success in our professional lives.

## Story 1

One such case study is that of Saba, a marketing executive who faced numerous setbacks in her career. Despite facing rejection after rejection, Saba never wavered in her belief in herself and her capabilities. Through sheer determination and hard work, she eventually landed a coveted position at a top advertising agency. Saba's story teaches us the importance of perseverance and never giving up, no matter how insurmountable the obstacles may seem.

## Story 2

Another inspiring example is that of Aman, a software engineer who struggled with imposter syndrome for years. Despite feeling like he didn't belong in his industry, Aman refused to let self-doubt hold him back. Through a combination of therapy, self-reflection, and seeking mentorship, Aman was able to overcome his insecurities and excel in his field. Aman's story shows us the power of mindset and the importance of seeking support when facing challenges.

## Story 3

The story of Mala, a business owner who faced bankruptcy early in her career, is another testament to the resilience of the human spirit. Instead of letting failure define her, Mala used it as a learning opportunity to reassess her business strategies and pivot in a new direction. Through hard work and determination, Mala was able to turn her business around and achieve even greater success than before. Mala's story teaches us that failure is not the end, but rather a stepping stone to greater achievements.

These case studies are my coachees, and I am the **CODE (THE TRANSFORMATION COACH).** These transformed success stories serve as powerful reminders that failure is not the end of the road, but rather a temporary setback on the path to success.

By adopting a growth mindset, seeking support when needed, and never giving up on our dreams, we too can crack the failure code and achieve our professional goals.

Let these stories inspire and motivate you to push through obstacles and reach new heights in your career.

## Sustaining Success Through Continued Growth and Development

In order to sustain success in your professional journey, it is essential to embrace continued growth and development. The key to avoiding complacency and ensuring ongoing success is to constantly seek out new opportunities for learning and improvement.

By investing in your personal and professional development, you are setting yourself up for long-term success and fulfillment.

Remember, success is not a destination but a journey, and it is important to keep moving forward.

One of the cornerstones of sustaining success is understanding and implementing **THE FAILURE CODE.**

This success formula ensures that you never fail, but rather learn and grow from your setbacks.

By reframing failure as an opportunity for growth and development, you can overcome obstacles and achieve even greater success in the future.

Embracing **THE FAILURE CODE** empowers you to approach challenges with a positive mindset and a determination to succeed no matter what.

Personal development is a crucial aspect of sustaining success. By continually working on yourself and your skills, you can adapt to the changing demands of the professional world and stay ahead of the curve. Whether it is through further education, training, or self-improvement practices, investing in your personal development is an investment in your future success.

Remember, growth is a continuous process, and it is important to always be striving for improvement.

Overcoming obstacles is a natural part of any professional journey, but how you respond to these challenges is what sets you apart.

By maintaining a positive mindset and a strong sense of motivation, you can overcome any obstacle that comes your way.

Remember, setbacks are not failures but opportunities for growth and development.

By approaching obstacles with a sense of determination and resilience, you can turn challenges into stepping stones towards even greater success.

So, sustaining success through continued growth and development is essential for working professionals who want to achieve their full potential.

By embracing **THE FAILURE CODE**, investing in personal development, overcoming obstacles, and maintaining a positive mindset, you can ensure that your success is not just temporary but long-lasting.

Remember, success is a journey, not a destination, and it is up to you to keep moving forward and striving for greatness.

■■

## EMBRACING FAILURE AS A STEPPING STONE TO SUCCESS

Finally, I would say embracing failure as a stepping stone to success is a crucial mindset shift that all working professionals must adopt in order to reach their full potential.

The journey to success is not always smooth sailing, and setbacks and failures are inevitable along the way.

However, it is how we choose to respond to these challenges that ultimately determines our success. By viewing failure as a valuable learning experience and an opportunity for growth, we can turn obstacles into stepping stones towards our goals.

**THE FAILURE CODE** offers a success formula that never fails - the key is to embrace failure, learn from it, and use it as a catalyst for growth and success.

By reframing our perspective on failure, we can unlock our full potential and achieve our goals with greater resilience and determination.

Personal development is a lifelong journey, and failure is an essential part of that process. By facing our fears and stepping out of our comfort zones, we can push past our limitations and achieve greatness.

Overcoming obstacles is a skill that all successful professionals must master.

By embracing failure as a natural part of the journey, we can develop the resilience and grit needed to overcome any challenge that comes our way. With the right mindset and motivation, we can turn setbacks into opportunities for growth and success.

By viewing failure as a temporary setback rather than a permanent defeat, we can stay focused on our goals and continue moving forward with confidence and determination.

In the end, success is not about avoiding failure, but about learning how to bounce back from it stronger and more determined than ever.

By embracing failure as a stepping stone to success, we can unlock our full potential and achieve our dreams with confidence and resilience.

**THE FAILURE CODE** is a powerful tool that can help working professionals navigate the ups and downs of their career with grace and determination.

By adopting the principles of **THE FAILURE CODE**, we can turn obstacles into opportunities and transform our failures into stepping stones towards success.

■■■

# BOOKS BY THE AUTHOR

## MY SCHOOL "MY FATHER": EVERYDAY PARENTING

This book is to bring back the quality time which parents can spend with their children, because by spending that time and interacting with them on a daily basis, they can build them into responsible and thoughtful human beings.

This book revolves around conversations between a father-son duo on various topics they witness in their daily life. The story's setting is that of a middle-class family of four.

The father Mr. Rama Krishnan Nair is working in a consumer durable company. They are natively from the state of Kerala but settled in Delhi from the past 20 years. Daughter, Smitha has recently graduated from a popular city school and is looking forward to higher studies abroad. Son, Prashantan is in the high school and is an extremely inquisitive child. The father-son duo often gets into discussions where the son is always curious to know about things, even about the ones which should be of no concern to him.

Mr. Nair by his own unique style of parenting attempts to broaden his children's thought process. The conversations which happen, reflect a lot on the healthy relationship which this father-son duo share with each other and the confidence, the son continues to have on his father.

This is a daring attempt to bring back that culture of face to face discussions and conversations in a family to overcome the booming hazards of the monstrous electronic social world. Every conversation ends up with a question or a doubt in the mind of the child or an answer which the father is about to give.

This book is not a read –through work only but a workbook where any of the parents or the children can complete the conversation to check their human values quotient.

■■■

## I THINK I KNOW YOU...KARUNYA, DO I?

A suspenseful and beguiling romantic-thriller novel; a love story with breath-taking intricacies of plots that will keep readers guessing and leafing through the pages with excitement.

Karunya, a Hindu Delhi boy and Aasma, a Muslim Lucknow girl fall in love with each other as they battle against a series of bizarre events. They set out on an adventure trip to unravel a mystery that has made their life miserable in the past few months.

But instead of setting it right, they put themselves into more grave problems. Karunya and Aasma get shocked when they finally discover the reasons behind the troubles they were going through.

The country is under a devastating terrorist attack. The special task force is formed to capture the gang of terrorists. While the terrorists and the STF team get down to even each other, Karunya and Aasma, the protagonists of the story are busy decoding the mystery.

The romantic thriller keeps the reader guessing that one person among all the characters in the novel, who at the end is discovered to be part of the terrorist gang.

■■■

## MY SCHOOL "MY FATHER": EVERYDAY PARENTING

**(Hindi Edition)**

इस किताब का उदेश्य उस खूबसूरत समय को वापिस लाने का है , जिसे मा- बाप अपने बच्चों के साथ बिता सकें , क्यूंकी वह समय बच्चों के साथ रोज़ बिताने से , उन्हे ज़िम्मेदार और समझदार इंसान बनाया जा सकता है |

ये किताब एक पिता और पुत्र के बीच में होने वाले जीवन के भिन्न समस्याओं पर होने वाली चर्चाओ पर आधारित है |

इस कहानी में चार लोगों का एक परिवार है पिता, रामा कृष्णा नायर एक प्राइवेट कंपनी में काम करते हैं ये लोग मूल रूप से केरल के

निवासी हैं , पर पिछले २० सालों से दिल्ली में ही बसे हुए हैं बेटी स्मिता ने अभी-अभी अपनी बारवही की परीक्षा शहर के नामी स्कूल से पास की है और बेटे प्रशांतन ने हाइ स्कूल की परीक्षा दी है प्रशांतन एक बेहद्द ही जिज्ञासु बच्चा है |

पिता-पुत्र अक्सर किसी ना किसी विषय की चर्चा में पड़ जाते हैं पुत्र हमेशा कुछ नया जानने की इच्छा में अपने पिता के साथ विचार विमर्श में पड़ जाता है और पिता अपने अनोखे तरीकों से पुत्र को कुछ ना कुछ ऐसा समझाते हैं, जिससे की उसका सोचने का दायरा बढ़ता रहता है दोनो के बीच में होने वाली बातें , उनके गहरे रिश्ते को साफ़ दर्शाती है |

यह एक साहस भरी कोशिश है , जिससे आज के समाज के मा-बाप अपने बच्चों के साथ विचार -विमर्श की आदतों में पड़कर उन्हे आज के मॉडर्न समाज के एलेक्ट्रॉनिक उपकरणों से दूर रख पाने में समर्थ हो पाएँगे और जीवन के उन मूल्यों को सीखा पाएँगे जो उनके आने वाले जीवन संघर्ष में मददगार साबित होंगे |

■■■

## THAT SINFUL DAY

**Book 1 (Ajit Panicker's L. S. D)**

Kunal, a sales professional, is travelling for work on one of his office trips with his boss, Sudeep. Kunal is married and is a one-woman man. Sudeep is married, however, is a jerk of the highest order.

On their way to from Delhi to Jhansi, on the National highway, Sudeep, finds a young - sexy girl, looking for lift. He stops his blue Ciaz to help the girl in distress. Kunal was half asleep. But by the time he realized, the girl was already inside the car.

And what the heck, when Kunal tries peeping at her through the rear view mirror of the car, he gets the biggest shock of his life.

Keerti was sitting at the rear seat; his unfinished love story...the love story which abruptly ended fifteen years back.

Read the complete story to know more...

■■■

## ONE STRAIGHT DOUBT

**Book-2 (Ajit Panicker's L . S. D)**

One Straight Doubt is the second story of the title , L.S.D-Unconfessed Stories of Love, Lust and Treachery. It is a standalone short story and part of the L.S.D title, which is the first book in the bold series.

Manjari who had faced two failed relationships decides never to get married. That was something she wished but then life at times throw you into what you are dead against. She gets married. Into an arranged marriage, that too after two failed love relationships she finds it really difficult to settle down, especially with a husband who was busy round the clock. She doubts him of infidelity.

What does she do when she doubts her husband of infidelity? How bad were her two previous relationships that she decides never to get married? Whatever she does to fight back, right from the two failed relationships to the doubts of infidelity on her husband, becomes a life-changing story for her.

Read the complete story to know more...

■■■

## FAST FURIOUS LIES

**Book-3 (Ajit Panicker's L . S . D)**

Fast Furious Lies is the third story of the title, Ajit Panicker's L.S.D-Unconfessed Stories of Love, Lust and Treachery. It is a standalone short story and part of the L.S.D title, which is the first book as an anthology in the bold series.

Joy George, India's fastest formula-one racing car champion, was just few races away from being crowned as the world's number one F1 driver. A top notch Casanova, who could put any celebrity to shame with his philandering ways, was at the peak of his career, when something derails him completely.

Not only his personal life but also his flourishing career gets into a trouble. What happens to Joy, the king of Formula-One circuit that leads to his defame? What was it that makes him lose all his credibility? Was it his philandering adventures? Was it the competition? or Something else.

Read the complete story to know more...

■■■

## BANDIT LOVE ENTANGLE

**Book-4 (Ajit Panicker's L.S.D)**

Bandit Love Entangle is the fourth story of the anthology titled L.S.D~unconfessed stories of love, lust and treachery. L.S.D is a collection of ten such stories and the first book as an anthology of the bold series.

Jhumroo Devi who has been living as the Bandit Queen of Chambal, is in her mid-sixties, when her grandson, Raghvendra Singh gets into something she cannot disown. Raghu and Anjalika while completing their graduation get into a blood-shed, where Raghu comes handy in saving Anjalika's life. But Kabeera Singh, who loses yet again, gets into a do or die mode. He swears to square off the dues with the queen.

What happens after so many years that trigger a war-like situation between Jhumroo Devi and Kabeera Singh? How does Anjalika, a common college going girl get involved in this battle? How does Sumitra who succeeds in keeping her only Son, Raghvendra, away from the ravines of Chambal, fall into the trap, yet again after almost twenty years? Read the complete story to know more.

If you happen to love the story and my writing style, please leave a review using the link given in the book, at the end of the story.

■■■

# THE LOVE AND SEEK STORIES:
# A COLLECTION OF FOUR STORIES

**The Love and Seek Stories is a collection of four short stories.**

The protagonist in each of the stories tussles with their relationships in life. Each of them has a past that hounds them back into their present.

Kunal, a regular family man was leading a pretty happy life, when all of a sudden; a single day changed his life forever. Life turns strange and nasty when you expect the least. That's what a work-related trip did to him. Will he survive the situation?

Manjhari was happily enjoying her single status, after having decided not to marry for life. Her past relationships had left no room for any new one to bloom. But then circumstances lead her to marry a man who had a lustrous career and status, great enough to cajole her mother. About a few months into the marriage and doubt creeps into her mind, a doubt that changes her life forever. Does the doubt turn real and she gets hurt one more time?

Joy, a young man with a super cult status as a formula-1 car racing champion makes way to add another to his long list of girlfriends. What happens when this new girl enters his life? His habit or her presence, what will change his life and status?

Raghu, a young lad meets a new girl in college. The very day they meet in the college canteen, unexpected bloodshed happens. They run to save their lives and take shelter under one of the most dreadful dacoits of the country. How a girl who turns into his life minutes back changes his world, shaking his very existence and origins?

Read on to know more...

■■■

## PAY OR DIE

**(Ajit Panicker's L.S.D Book 5)**

Pay or Die is the fifth story of the book titled L.S.D - unconfessed stories of love, lust and treachery. L.S.D, is a collection of ten such stories, and the first book of the bold series.

In a tale of greed, deception, and family turmoil, Sneha's scheming family, led by a greedy doctor mother and a compelled father, takes center stage. As Sneha's younger brother, Sahil, battles drug addiction, Tarun, Son of the Business tycoon Samar Chopra, defies wealth and decides to become a doctor. How Sahil and Sneha cross paths? How Tarun's decision affects his father and his sister Monica? Who deceives whom to overpower each other?

Read to know more...

■■■

## MYSTERY OF THE MISTAKEN MYSTIC

**(SIVANNAH Book 1)**

Sivan the protagonist in this novel, who from being a poor, frail-looking, average loner guy turns into a super-rich business magnate.

Is it about how he goes through the various ups and downs in his life while continuing to make a mark for himself in this not so good world?

That is what you should watch out this novel for.

But what is the mystery then?

Is it mysticism, as the title suggests?

Is it a murder mystery?

Is it a thriller?

Is it magic realism?

The story starts while he is in college, how he meets the love of his life, Rakhi.

There is something that he finds that changes his life forever. Something you should read the novel to find out.

From a no-one to the one the world starts saluting, his journey as you read is inspiring but what is interesting is the mystery and suspense that develops half way through the book.

To know what is that mystery, read it till the very end. The suspense, thrill and the mystery with romance builds this story into a lively book you would cherish reading.

This is how the story starts...

Sivan sat on a carved antique chair, gazing out the window, shuddering every time a silver lightning flashed through the overcast sky. His hands held a strange-looking fountain pen, his fingers twirling it between them. His elbows rested on the table, right beside a small diary and a transparent unbreakable water bottle.

Without much sunlight that usually illuminated the room, he was forced to use a fluorescent study lamp and open the windows to let the cool breeze waft in. Lost in thoughts, his eyes kept its focus fixed on the lawn outside and at the tree outside the boundary line. At any other time, he would have been happier, but today, despite the charming weather, he felt depressed.

All of a sudden, the pen dropped to the floor. The sound would have made anyone break out of the trance and bend over to pick up the pen, but he did nothing of the sort. Instead, he pressed his temple from both sides – a sign of his unbearable pain. His day at the college had been awful. He could still feel the voices of his peers inside his head.

You are such a dumb ass. Horrible you look. Why don't you do something?

It is so embarrassing for us. Leave at once.

Who the hell would want to be your girlfriend? You are such a loser. Go get a makeover for yourself. His mind replayed the day's events in a loop. He saw himself stranded in a corner, hands folded as if to shield himself from the boisterous attacks they flung at him.

Read on to know more...

■■■

# BOSSOLOGY: HOW TO MANAGE YOUR BOSS

In "Bossology: How to Manage Your Boss," the author delves into the intricacies of navigating the complex dynamics between employees and their superiors. Recognizing that a successful professional relationship with one's boss is crucial for career advancement and job satisfaction, the book offers practical insights and strategies for effectively managing this pivotal connection.

The book begins by emphasizing all possible reasons why people leave companies, the impact of boss-driven departures on the company, and decoding the early departures under specific types of bosses.

Drawing on real-world examples and psychological insights, the author provides readers with a toolkit to decode their boss's behavior and adapt their approach accordingly.

A significant portion of the book is dedicated to the types of bosses we may face in our job roles. The author encourages readers to take initiative, anticipate their boss's needs, and contribute meaningfully to the team and organization's success. Through case studies and actionable tips, "Bossology" demonstrates how employees can position themselves as valuable assets, earning the trust and respect of their superiors.

The book majorly addresses the challenges of dealing with different types of bosses. It provides readers with strategies to handle conflicts diplomatically, seek constructive feedback, and turn challenging situations into opportunities for growth.

Additionally, "Bossology" explores the concept of upward management, empowering employees to express their career goals and seek mentorship from their supervisors.

The book takes you through the desired qualities of a good boss, the characteristics of a devastating boss, the crucial role of boss management in career progression, differences between a leader and a manager, a transforming boss, benefits of accommodating to boss's style of working, and steps to accommodate to boss's style of working.

Overall, **"BOSSOLOGY: How to Manage Your Boss"** is a comprehensive guide for employees seeking to enhance their relationships with supervisors and thrive in their careers. Whether you're a new hire looking to make a positive impression or a seasoned professional aiming for career advancement, this book provides practical strategies and timeless principles for mastering the art of managing up.

■■■

www.ingramcontent.com/pod-product-compliance
Ingram Content Group UK Ltd.
Pitfield, Milton Keynes, MK11 3LW, UK
UKHW020051200726
13845UKWH00056B/812

9 789334 149326